D1456840

THE
GREAT
GREEN
GOLD
RUSH

Compelling stories of gifted professionals who are on one
of the greatest rides in the history of free enterprise

KATHLEEN TRACY   MICHAEL CALDWELL

THE GREAT GREEN GOLD RUSH

ISBN: 978-0-9952593-1-7

Design and layout by Chris Mendoza
Writing by Kathleen Tracy and Michael Caldwell
Editing by Kathleen Tracy

Printed in the United States of America by Bang Printing

TABLE OF CONTENTS

PAGE

INTRODUCTION i

ARCVIEW GROUP 1

BLUEBIRD BOTANICALS 15

BLUM OAK. 29

CANNALINE PACKAGING 43

FOREVER FLOWERING GREENHOUSES 57

GREEN FLOWER MEDIA. 73

HARBORSIDE HEALTH CENTER. 89

HOBAN LAW GROUP. 105

JDW, LLC. 121

MEDICALLY CORRECT 135

NEW FRONTIER 151

OAKSTERDAM UNIVERSITY. 165

US HEMP WHOLESALE. 179

WHOOPI & MAYA 193

WILLIE NELSON RESERVE 207

INTRODUCTION

The best entrepreneurs have a knack for looking around social, technological, or cultural corners to identify coming trends or opportunities. And today the biggest bullseye is the coming green rush. As of late 2016, 26 states had legalized medical marijuana; eight of those plus the District of Columbia have also legalized adult use.

Research firm ArcView Group reports that legal marijuana is the fastest-growing industry in the United States. Fortune magazine estimated that sales in 2016 would reach $6.7 billion. By 2020 that number is expected to exceed $20 billion. In 2015, Colorado reaped $88 million in taxes on medical marijuana—more than double of what the state collected from alcohol. The economic potential of cannabis—both industrial the hemp and marijuana—is massive. Couple that with changing public attitudes that show most Americans favor legalization and you have fertile ground for innovators and forward thinkers to make their entrepreneurial mark.

Cannabis has been grown in the US since colonial times. In the 1800s drugs like cannabis, opiates, and cocaine were freely available at pharmacies. Cannabis was sold in liquid form and as hashish. It was also a common ingredient in numerous medicines. In 1862, *Vanity Fair* ran an advertisement for hashish candy to treat nervousness and melancholy. The ad called the candy "a pleasurable and harmless stimulant. Under its influence, all classes seem to gather new inspiration and energy."

During this time hemp was also a popular industrial material, its fiber used in rope and ships' riggings. But political agendas and social perceptions changed in the early twentieth century. After the Mexican Revolution started in 1920, there was a surge of immigrants flooding into states like Texas and Louisiana. As always, immigrants bring elements of their culture; for the Mexicans that included cannabis as a medicine and relaxant.

The Mexican immigrants called cannabis *marihuana*, a word few Americans associated with cannabis. Anti-immigrant politicians and members of the press spread xenophobic rhetoric about Mexicans, using their marijuana use as proof of their danger to our society. The irony being more Americans than not had products in their medicine cabinet with marijuana in it.

El Paso, TX, outlawed marijuana, giving them cause to search, detain, and deport Mexican immigrants for breaking the law. It became a national strategy for controlling immigrants and other minorities. In the 1930s "experts" claimed marijuana caused men of color to become violent and sexually aggressive toward white women. That frightened the public and paved the way for laws targeting cannabis.

One of the most notorious, anti-marijuana crusaders was Harry J. Anslinger, a former assistant commissioner of the Prohibition Bureau who headed the U.S. Treasury Department's Narcotics Bureau from 1930 to 1962. Playing on the public's fears, he pressed for uniform anti-narcotics legislation in all then-48 states.

When testifying before Congress, Anslinger presented a litany of murders and rapes allegedly committed by people high on marijuana. In an article he wrote titled "Marijuana, Assassin of Youth," he stated: "How many murders, suicides, robberies, criminal assaults, holdups, burglaries and deeds of maniacal insanity it causes each year can only be conjectured."

Anslinger also lobbied for the Marijuana Tax Act of 1937, which effectively banned the use and sale of cannabis, and worked to discredit any research that contradicted his views on the danger of cannabis and other drugs or disputed the effectiveness of prohibition. When the New York Academy of Medicine prepared a report in 1944 concluding that marijuana was only a mild intoxicant, Anslinger lobbied the American Journal of Psychiatry to publish an article refuting the claims. He also tried to prevent publication of a joint American Bar Association-American Medical Association study that argued penalties for cannabis possession were too harsh. Anslinger's perspective was that heroin, cocaine, or marijuana were all essentially the same: addictive and dangerous.

The cultural revolution of the mid-1960s brought cannabis to a new generation who wanted to turn on, tune in, drop out. For most youth, smoking pot was harmless fun and the legal penalties for cannabis came under scrutiny. It was one thing to lock up minorities and immigrants, but the American public wasn't eager to lock up a generation of college students for what now seemed like a victimless crime. Hippie activists decried the sentencing penalties, and major publications and newspapers questioned why it remained illegal.

But the government remained dogged. After the Marijuana Tax Act of 1937 was ruled unconstitutional decades later, Congress passed the Controlled Substances Act in the 1970s, which established schedules for ranking substances by their dangerousness and potential for addiction. Cannabis was placed in the most restrictive category, Schedule I. It was supposed to be temporary until a commission could determine where it belonged.

President Nixon's the Schafer Commission declared that

marijuana should not be in Schedule I and questioned designating it an illicit substance at all. They sided with proponents of decriminalizing cannabis who rejected the argument that there wasn't enough research to approve medicinal or recreational use, pointing out the plant has been used safely by humans for around five thousand years.

However, Nixon rejected the commission's recommendations, and as of 2016, the FDA continued to classify cannabis a Schedule I substance. While the federal government clung to its outdated policies, progressive voters defied federal law and passed state initiatives legalizing cannabis for medical use, which has proven an economic, humanitarian, and wellness success. The effort to legalize recreational use is quickly gaining traction.

With public acceptance comes business opportunities. The current generation of cannabis entrepreneurs and trailblazers, as represented in this book, is a diverse group. Some hail from families who have cultivated cannabis for generations. Some discovered the benefits of cannabis during an illness, after an accident, or when caring for a loved one and became passionate about helping others improve their health and well-being through dispensaries, edibles, and products—ventures all designed to improve the users' quality of life. Others have identified needs unique to this industry—greenhouses, public education, packaging, specialized legal assistance, and medical research.

Most are unapologetic users who enjoy cannabis in a variety of ways: smoking, vaping, edibles, and tinctures. And all believe the value and benefits of cannabis—from medical marijuana to industrial hemp—remains largely untapped and its potential is limited only by our imagination.

While it may not be the ambrosia of the Greek gods, it may be the closest thing to it for us mortals here on earth.

ARCVIEW GROUP

This is not your grandfather's cannabis business. With each state that adopts some form of legalization, cannabis becomes less outlaw and more mainstream. Perhaps nothing is more reflective of that than the ArcView Group, which brings together investors and cannabis entrepreneurs to "meet the expanding and changing needs of responsible cultivators, dispensaries, and customers nationwide."

As of late 2016, ArcView Group has amassed 550 investor members that have invested $85 million in 130 companies. Co-founder and chief executive officer Troy Dayton says ArcView was founded to facilitate growth. "There was a gap in the process. Companies in the cannabis industry often had great ideas but had a difficult time reaching investors. They didn't know how to give an effective pitch, or they didn't have the skillset to take things to the next level. Or they didn't know the things that make a company investable such as assembling a team with great credentials and having a focused plan—too many entrepreneurs in the cannabis industry try to do too much.

"On the other side, I saw these high-net-worth people, many who were just donating in hopes of changing laws because they simply cared about the cause. Those investors were becoming interested in this industry they were helping to start, but didn't understand it either."

To bring both sides together, Troy teamed up with Steve DeAngelo of Harborside Health Center in March 2010 to launch ArcView Group. For Troy, it was the culmination of years as a cannabis activist.

It's not unusual for the stirring of political or social activism to take root in high school or college, as the insular confines of childhood expand and evolve into a young adulthood's worldview. Less common is to see the light after being punk'd. Troy says his first experience smoking marijuana as a teenager in suburban Hillsborough, New Jersey, during the mid-1990s wasn't just memorable; it was life changing.

"When I was a senior high school, I tried cannabis for the first time with some friends of mine. We were in the parking lot of a building that looked like a warehouse, and in the middle of me consuming it, a security guard car, with light flashing, pulled up next to us. The guard got out and put me in handcuffs. He took me to the front of the building," back when they still had pay phones, "and said: *You can either call your parents or you can call the cops. I* opted to call my mom. In the middle of dialing, he put his finger on the receiver."

The whole "arrest" was an elaborate prank.

"My friends came pouring into the room laughing and cracking up that they had made this great joke." Troy wasn't quite as amused. "It was kind of a jerk move on their part. But what they didn't realize was that they created an activist that day because that experience made me realized how many people didn't have the benefit of it being a joke that for them. At that time, nearly a million people every year were being arrested on cannabis charges—for real. I thought it was crazy that people were being punished for consuming it. It just turned my stomach. My friends' prank inspired my sense of justice that marijuana prohibition was wrong, and I wanted to change it."

Troy has described himself as a credible rebel, which he defines as someone who "identifies injustices and supports the misunderstood underdog." He took that rebel perspective with him to American University in Washington, DC, where he pursued his interest in cannabis activism. "Arnold Trebach, who was the father of the modern drug policy reform movement a professor there and I took his Drugs, Alcohol, and Society class as a freshman in 1995."

Convinced the government had overstepped its authority by making cannabis illegal, he became involved in the cannabis legalization movement. During his freshman year, Troy started volunteering for the newly-formed Marijuana Policy Project and interned at the Drug Reform Coordination Network. He also established a National Organization for the Reform of Marijuana Laws (NORML) chapter on the campus. A year later California passed Prop 21, becoming the first state to legalize medical marijuana, giving activists like Troy a sense of instant gratification and validation that change was in the air.

During his senior year, Troy also co-founded the National Students for Sensible Drug Policy, which is now on more than two hundred college campuses. But after college Troy initially drifted away from activism to pursue a career in the IT world during the dot-com boom of the late 1990s at a digital media start-up called Zoom Culture.

"We all thought we're going to be billionaires," he laughs. "But that company eventually went bust in 2000 like the rest of them. After that, I worked on drug policy reform for a while as a fundraiser."

His next venture was in renewable energy in with some former coworkers from Zoom Culture. Troy went to Boulder, Colorado, and started Renewable Choice Energy, which launched in January 2002 to provide customized clean energy products and services to the commercial, industrial, and institutional sector. As the national sales manager, Troy co-created and managed the residential sales program and co-created a Fortune 500 national sales program. The company quickly found its niche and has since become an award-winning, major player in renewable energy.

But Troy couldn't leave cannabis activism behind. Or maybe it's more accurate to say cannabis kept calling him back. "Renewable energy was booming, and I was right there for it. I had a chance to make a play there, but I kept getting called to work on drug policy. And it felt like that was why I was put on earth. Although every time I got called, I'd say to myself: *You know, I'm really signing up for a life of poverty.*"

Troy ended up leaving Renewable Choice Energy after a little more than a year and in May 2003 went to work for the Interfaith Drug Policy Initiative, which organized religious leaders, congregations, and denominations to support various drug policy reform. He stayed there nearly four years.

Troy says he assumed, "I was giving up on riches and whatnot. Multiple times as I grew up and in my career, I kept on having to choose between changing the world and making a lot of money. I thought I had to choose between them. It wasn't until around 2009 that I realized all our efforts to change cannabis laws was creating the next big business boom; I didn't have to decide whether to change the world or to make a lot of money through business. I could do both. Once that occurred to me, it became very clear that the lessons we learned in the renewable energy industry were going to be valuable in the cannabis industry."

One of those lessons was that just because you care about something doesn't make it profitable and doesn't make it grow. "Renewable energy did not become a fast-growing industry until there were profitable business models associated with it. Until the hippies who cared about it could convince people who didn't care about it that it made sense from a business standpoint. That's what ultimately spread it." It is also similar, he says, to the organic foods industry.

"I think we see the same thing happen with cannabis. If you look at renewable energy, it has spread across the world because people figured out models to make it profitable. Organic foods have spread across the country—and the world—for the same reason. I think cannabis legalization is going to spread across the world as well because we're finding ways to create a profitable, responsible, and politically engaged cannabis industry. That's going to move the political needle."

Troy points out these industries didn't come from corporate America. "Those are great examples of where the hippies keep being right," he says with a laugh. "It's no mistake that some of the best business ideas of the last twenty or thirty years have come from the counterculture, people who are inspired to see the world change in a particular way and then spread those ideas through the development of profitable, mainstream business models."

From 2007 to 2009, Troy was the Marijuana Policy Project's lead fundraiser in California. By that time, MPP was—and still is—the largest organization in the US focusing solely on ending marijuana prohibition. "I was based out in Northern California with the goal of talking to high net worth individuals who could be major donors for our efforts. Also, I was charged with going out and talking to the burgeoning new legal cannabis industry.

"I was raising money from a lot of high-net-worth individuals who simply cared about changing the law. They weren't in it for business. I also raised money from dispensaries, people who were donating in part because they were committing civil disobedience and cared about protecting themselves. It was seeing those two groups of people and realizing that one side wanted to grow their businesses and expand but didn't understand how, while the other side had made their money in other investments and thought they knew something about cannabis but instead started making really terrible investments," he laughs.

The better he got to know individuals from both sides of the cannabis financial coin, the more he realized there was a fundamental leadership gap in the industry at that time. The need to take the industry to a new level of growth, profitability, and sustainability led to Troy teaming with Harborside Health Center founder Steve DeAngelo to start the ArcView Group in 2010. The start-up's early customer base were people Troy and Steve knew from their other work in the industry, so they started with name recognition and credibility.

While the company now has a very focused vision, in the early years it struggled to find its identity. "When we started, we weren't quite sure of what we were going to do," Troy admits, "so we did a bunch of different things. For example, we created a mobile app for dispensaries, which at the time was very revolutionary and we sold a bunch of those. Most of the apps at that time were dispensary finder apps. But the dispensaries didn't want an app that would help people find other dispensaries. So we said: *Okay, let's make an app for each dispensary*. And we sold a lot of those."

But the primary objective, Troy says, was to be an incubator, meaning a firm that fosters early-stage companies through its development until the start-up has sufficient resources to function on its own. "We were going to be the Y Combinator of cannabis," he says, referring to a well-known digital incubator. "But this was 2010, mind you, centuries ago in cannabis terms, right? So there were no people willing to do that. We wanted to create CannaLand, which was going to be like Epcot Center for cannabis but we couldn't get any traction with that."

They tried several ideas that were essentially too ahead of their time to generate enough interest to pursue. Then in late 2011 they put on the first ArcView Investor Network Forum. "It included about ten investors and two companies giving them their pitches," Troy recalls. "That began the ArcView Investor Network."

But it took a while to build momentum, and at one point in 2012, ArcView almost went out of business because of a government crackdown on cannabis. "I was homeless for some time," he recalls. "I was living on people's couches. Nobody was interested in investment during that time, and I had lost a lot of faith in what we were doing. In fact, I had begun to consider building another type of career."

Troy says he persevered because of Steve's steadfast passion for their cause. "Steve never wavered in his vision, commitment, and belief that ArcView would become what it is today. He stayed encouraged that the cannabis industry would grow and build into something pivotal for the world. I admire him for his unbelievable sense of vision in addition to his willingness and effectiveness when it comes to inspiring people. Having been the recipient of that inspiration means a lot to me. I'm very grateful to Steve and have learned a lot from him."

That dark time gave way to optimism, toward the end of 2012 when polls showed voters in Colorado and Washington were likely going to pass ballot initiatives to legalize cannabis for adult recreational use. "At that point, people started calling again. I thought that once those propositions passed, the phone would start ringing off the hook. While business did get better, it didn't really go nuts until January of 2014 when Colorado started selling cannabis to adults. They hadn't just passed the law; they had implemented it. Adults were standing in line buying cannabis from stores. After that, we couldn't answer the phones fast enough. We ballooned from a very small number of members to hundreds in just a few months. It was unbelievable. Then in April 2013, we were on the cover of *Fortune* magazine. And that was a real game changer for us as well."

Today, the ArcView Group offers several services besides its Investor Network including Arcview Market Research, CanopyBuilder, and Cannasure Insurance Services to help "the next generation of cannabis-related businesses." Troy says those cannabis-related businesses run the gamut.

"We've got hemp companies, we've got pharmaceutical companies, we have point-of-sale software companies, social networks for cannabis consumers, dispensaries, product manufacturers, cultivation equipment, nutrients—you name it."

But for as much as cannabis activists have achieved in general—

and the ArcView Group has grown in particular—Troy warns against complacency because there is still much to do.

"We started ArcView with the belief that if we could build a credible, responsible, and profitable industry, we would ultimately end cannabis prohibition. Currently on of our biggest goals is to end federal marijuana prohibition by 2020. But, it is critical that we inspire people to donate to these efforts. The media has done a great job of giving this issue a sense of inevitability, which is a dangerous thing because it's only a *sense* of inevitability. It is not inevitable. It's only inevitable if we raise a certain amount of money to pass ballot initiatives and that amount surpasses anything we've raised for our issues previously."

Troy notes that supporters poured more money into promoting Prop 64, California's recreational adult use initiative than has ever been spent before. And there are several other states now looking to legalize cannabis for either medical, recreational, or both, and those efforts need both money and boots on the ground.

"The most important thing is for people to continue actively supporting the cause," Troy says. "Whether you're a cannabis-related entrepreneur or you simply care about the cause, we cannot afford to rest on our laurels because we're so close to achieving our goal. The most dangerous thing we can do is to see the positive headlines and believe the job is done. We've got to keep fighting."

Troy recalls how when he first became a cannabis activist people laughed at him and said legalization was a pipe dream. "Then almost overnight the story changed, and now everybody says it's inevitable. It wasn't hopeless then, and it's not inevitable now. The one thing that was needed then and is needed now is people's dollars—and actions. If it turns your stomach that we live in a society where there are still hundreds of thousands of people being arrested for possessing a substance that is safer than alcohol, I invite your participation. I also recommend that you start by becoming a member of the Marijuana Policy Project and sign up for their local state and federal alerts."

While Troy says he's excited that ArcView has created "an engine that can support itself as well as support the development of both jobs and wealth," his long-term goal is to ensure that the company "keeps providing the most value that it can while also providing a light for people to remain committed to the cause."

His commitment to ending cannabis prohibition notwithstanding, as he has matured as an activist and a human being, Troy says he has learned the value of me-time. "I think the biggest mistake many entrepreneurs make, myself included, is allowing your business to consume you. For me, it happened earlier in my career. I found myself getting stressed out and losing sleep, worrying about payroll or some news story I read. That stress can take its toll on an entrepreneur. So now I try to have a better work-life balance. What my business needs is for me to be calm, spacious, and thinking clearly, not killing myself under massive amounts of work.

"Making the shift from an early stage company to a mid-stage company and owning that piece of the leadership puzzle is really important for entrepreneurs. I would go so far as to say that it is just as important for early stage entrepreneurs as well. If I could do it all over again, I would not have sacrificed my happiness to make it happen. I would have found a way to do both. That's my biggest advice to entrepreneurs. It's going to be hard, it's going to be a struggle, but you don't need to sacrifice personal happiness to make it happen."

Regardless of how successful his entrepreneurial efforts have been or will be, Troy remains driven by his sense of justice. "It is important to remember the real societal impact positive legislation could have on a global scale. There are people out there still sitting in prison—not just in the US, but all over the world—for this plant. We owe it to them to do this right and to not miss a single opportunity to end marijuana prohibition anywhere on earth. We need to honor the people who have made great sacrifices because of these terrible laws. I want to make sure that this is a crowning achievement of for both the cannabis industry as well as people around the world who care about the movement."

BLUEBIRD BOTANICALS

Brandon Beatty admits that growing up he always believed that one day he would be an advocate of some sort. "I've always had that inkling to do something big, to do something important, to make a real difference," Brandon says. "I suspect we all have those feelings, but it was particularly strong in me, that deep craving to do something big and meaningful and truly helpful. To be an advocate for some greater good. I just didn't have cannabis in mind," he chuckles, "but it's given me satisfaction beyond what I could have expected."

Brandon is the founder of Denver-based Bluebird Botanicals, which sells cannabis-based supplements. Born and raised in New Jersey, he moved to Colorado in 2009.

"It was just on a whim actually," he says. "I drove out here with a friend. I was in my early twenties and thought: *Let's just have fun*. It was an open-ended adventure, and I had no idea what was to come. I had a friend who lived out here and invited me to stay for a little while until I got my feet on solid ground."

Brandon quickly found a job working at an herbal supplement company in Boulder. "It's an online company that did very highly refined extractions of plants, and the extractions would be in oil form. They had more than one hundred different types of plants that they were extracting."

After a couple of years, Brandon was promoted to head manager, where he learned how to run an online company. "Especially one that dealt with herbal extracts in particular," he says. "For a period of time, my boss wasn't around that much, so I got really comfortable with the responsibility. It got to where I was very much doing what an owner would do. I was writing checks, negotiating and making deals, overseeing sales, and making sure daily operations were smooth. At a certain point it dawned on me: *I should be doing this for myself...*"

Brandon says he had the passion for being an entrepreneur and the confidence in his managerial skill set and business knowledge, so after five years of managing the Boulder-based herbal company, he quit and set out to start his own venture. Initially, it was a general herbal, nutritional company.

"It wasn't meant to be a hemp-centric company," he explains, "although it's evolved to be that over the years. The first time I heard of cannabidiol (CBD) was in 2009."

CBD is a naturally occurring component of industrial hemp/ cannabis. Hemp refers to strains of *Cannabis sativa* that have been bred specifically for industrial use in clothing, construction, natural plastic, oils, topical ointments, and a growing variety of other purposes. Most people associate the word cannabis with marijuana, which refers to strains of *Cannabis sativa* and other cannabis species specifically bred for flowers containing THC, the chemical substance that produces the drug high. By using selective breeding techniques, cannabis breeders have managed to create varieties with high levels of CBD—which is not psychoactive—and next to zero levels of THC.

"I saw that and realized: *Okay, there are dozens of other cannabinoids that aren't psychoactive,*" Brandon recalls. "And they are completely legal if you derive them from industrial hemp. When I discovered this, a light bulb went off, and it immediately became clear to me that CBD would soon be just as recognized as THC. I saw this huge opportunity, and I thought: *Okay, this is clearly going to happen and I can choose to be a part of it and be on the ground floor, or not.* I just had that foresight much earlier than most people. I believe we were the very first private company to sell hemp derived 'CBD oil' nationwide, which was in 2013."

At the time, it was a revolutionary and somewhat brave

endeavor. "We didn't have the safety in numbers that other people are now getting in the industry," he says. "Now there are hundreds of companies that sell cannabinoid oils, but I didn't have that industry support four years ago. We went out on a limb, and it has paid off."

Part of the challenge Brandon faced was educating the public. "Five years ago, when I was telling people that CBD will be a household term within a matter of years, hardly anyone knew what CBD was. Less than one percent of the population was aware of the chemical CBD, although it's been a major constituent of all hemp and cannabis for thousands of years."

One of those people unaware of CBD was Brandon's dad, who is Bluebird's main attorney. "Like most people, he wasn't aware of CBD. When he looked into it, he was able to confirm and verify that if you source it from certain countries in particular ways, import it properly, and market it like we do, then it's legal. He was able to confirm the strategy that we'd developed to sell hemp extracts as dietary supplements. I don't think he was necessarily concerned or excited at first because he probably didn't think the company would take off like it did. That was my first time starting a company, and I didn't have a business background."

The rules governing hemp are complex. The Controlled Substances Act of 1970 banned the industrial cultivation of hemp by classifying marijuana as a schedule 1 drug. That was the first time that the federal government created legislation that essentially grouped hemp and marijuana into the same category.

"Yeah, there are a lot of nuances in my sub-industry with its own specific set of regulations and hurdles that we're dealing with. That is why we have three attorneys," Brandon says. "One is just for cannabis and hemp regulation. One is just for Federal Drug Administration compliance with marketing our products."

Some of the regulations include prohibitions on testimonials or intimating that CBD has any specific health benefits. Brandon points out those same rules cover all dietary supplements. "But a lot of people in the nutritional and supplement industry do it anyway. The FDA doesn't always write them letters or officially object to it, but it is against the regulations. Probably over half the supplement companies in America are breaking FDA regulations with their marketing," he laughs. "But the FDA only has so much money and so many people, so they try to target the biggest public health threats and put those at the top of their priority list."

Bluebird Botanical's third attorney is Brandon's dad. "He is our general attorney for contracts and daily purposes. And he's also like a mentor for me. He graduated at the top of his class from Harvard Law School, so he's an incredibly smart guy. In retrospect, it was a huge educational asset for me growing up with him. He also owns a law firm, Kent, Beatty & Gordon, so as a business owner and commercial attorney he's there to provide me with tons of advice."

Brandon says his goals were modest when he started Bluebird. "I thought hopefully it'll take off and maybe a few years from now we'll be making a decent amount of money to make a career out of, but very quickly we started making millions of dollars in sales within our first calendar year. It kicked off so quickly and became a much bigger deal than I think anyone was expecting."

Brandon says he started Bluebird with four thousand dollars in cash and about five credit cards, which in retrospect he believes was taking on more risk than was necessary. "We had to immediately recoup the cost to pay off those credit cards fast. And so there was a lot of pressure to make immediate sales right at the beginning of the company. Managing the extremely rapid growth of the company with limited startup funds was very challenging. We had to constantly increase our inventory, space, processes, and team of employees, and with minimal cash, this was like walking on a tightrope for the first six months. Eventually, our cash flow became significant enough to accommodate the many moving pieces and growth of the company."

Not having any contacts in the cannabis industry, Brandon simply went online and started searching hemp farms and hemp producers around the world. "I quickly discovered that there are lots of high-quality hemp cultivars being grown in massive quantities in Europe."

Brandon says Bluebird has actively avoided Chinese grown hemp because of potential pollution issues and labor concerns. "A lot of the manufacturing facilities in China pay their employees very, very little. Bluebird is a very holistic, progressive, and health-oriented company, so we try not to support anything that's hurting people or the planet."

After researching his options, Brandon selected a co-op of hemp farmers in Denmark, Lithuania, and Germany. "It's a group of farmers that share the same seeds. We would get the raw hemp extract delivered in bulk to America, and then we would use that raw ingredient to formulate our different blends in my kitchen for roughly the first month. But then, very quickly we started using a shared kitchen space here in Colorado where we would do all our FDA-compliant manufacturing."

The company was growing so quickly month-to-month that they needed more lab time than the shared kitchen had available. "That made it really hard to manufacture on time and keep the product on the shelves as we were growing so rapidly. So we built out our own compliant, state-of-the-art lab and a production and shipping facility. We have a $40,000 high-pressure liquid chromatography machine and a $100,000 CO_2 extractor among other pieces of equipment to test and produce our products. So that's where we're doing all our manufacturing now. It's been an evolving growthprocess since the beginning."

Brandon credits the company's growth to a combination of marketing and grass roots word of mouth. "There's a huge amount of word of mouth; it's really big for us. We spend more than $30,000 a month in marketing as well. We've spent tons of money in acquiring new clients. But once a client has bought a product, most of the time they are extremely happy with it and then they'll go and tell everybody they know about it. Every single family member will hear about it, every neighbor, every friend, they'll even tell people in line at the grocery store—and with good reason. Our products are changing lives every day. And as a company we always do our very best to provide our clients with the best service and as much care and respect as possible, and I think that goes a much longer way than most people would think."

Brandon estimates it took about a year to position Bluebird to where it would be competitive for years to come. Many entrepreneurs have a hard time delegating as their company grows. Brandon says he "very naturally delegated as the need arose. We now have Michael Harinen as our head of marketing, so at this point I'm only involved in marketing to a certain extent, not spearheading that program. We also have a full-time treasurer and co-owner, Wendy Black, who also deals with a lot of the time-consuming Humans Relations matters. We also have a Vice President, Quinatzin De La

Torre, who's my right-hand man. And we also have an operations manager at our lab, David Sommer, who has a background in food production and kitchen compliance, and a handful of other talented lab technicians working for us as well. We also recently hired a guy, who specializes in data and analytics, to help with our marketing and financial abilities. At our headquarters we've built an outstanding customer service and sales team. Most of the people at Bluebird were friends before its inception. We're like a family. I feel I have delegated well so far, and it's made it much easier to deal with the big picture things. Now I can strategize for the company and not be so caught up in the day to day, focusing more on strategic partnerships and alliances, political endeavors that will benefit the hemp industry, long-term brand strategy, diversifying by investing in other sectors of the industry, etc."

Some of those bigger picture items include promoting the use of marijuana. To that end, Brandon is currently an investor with the ArcView Group, which was founded in 2010 to provide cannabis funding to build the legal cannabis industry in the United States. Brandon says as a group the organization has supplied more than $70 million in marijuana funding. He is also investing personally in the cannabis industry.

"My plan is to invest in a handful of marijuana companies over the next couple of years, form some strong partnerships, and diversify because the cannabis industry is huge. Bluebird also donated over $50,000 to different organizations to pass positive cannabis legislation last year."

Brandon was an original co-founder and the original treasurer of the Industrial Hemp Research Foundation, a Colorado-based nonprofit that gives funding and support to local universities including Colorado State University, Colorado University, and Adams State University for hemp research and to develop even more uses for it. He is also an advisor to the National Hemp Association, another Colorado nonprofit that supports all aspects of the hemp industry. Currently, their main project is trying to pass the Industrial Hemp Farming Act.

The Bluebird website notes: "Currently the US is the largest importer and consumer of hemp products, and we're the only industrialized nation that doesn't grow it. This federal legislation will pave the way for industrial hemp to be produced, processed, and distributed nationwide—in all capacities, without restriction. There are many uses for hemp: rebuilding soil; making textiles and super-capacitors for batteries from the fiber; producing paper products from the pulp; using the stalk to create car door panels and other automobile parts; hemp bio-fuel; and creating food, beverages, and other nutritional products from hemp seeds and oil, to name a few."

Brandon says while there is a host of various legislations that would benefit the hemp industry, S.2237—introduced in November

2015 by Senator Bernie Sanders—would have the most impact. "It would not just reschedule cannabis, but it would completely take it off the DEA's Controlled Substances Act. And that would cover both marijuana and industrial hemp. But it has zero sponsors in the House, zero sponsors in the Senate, so it's not exactly feasible to pass it in the near future. But the Industrial Hemp Farming Act has sixty-nine cosponsors in the House and fourteen cosponsors in the Senate right now."

In April 2016 about 25 cannabis industry stakeholders traveled to Washington DC, and Brandon says they decided to form a coalition to fight for all positive things for the hemp industry. "One thing we'll be doing is trying to pass the Industrial Hemp Farming Act, which we've been raising funds and already lobbying for. We hope to pass this bill and make it law. Hopefully, next year at the latest would be nice. It would affect the hemp industry as a whole because it would mean anybody in America could grow, process and sell hemp. We wouldn't have to get it from Europe. We could, at that point, extract locally grown commercial hemp from Colorado and sell it nationwide. And then the USDA might approve hemp as a viable crop and start giving out loans and grants and certifying it as an organic crop, too. That would be huge for the American hemp industry."

Another obstacle the coalition will attempt to address are the FDA issues the industry is dealing with. For example, the FDA in 2015 stated that CBD could not be marketed as a dietary supplement. According to the FDA, "There is an exception if the substance was marketed as a dietary supplement or as a conventional food before the new drug investigations were authorized; however, based on available evidence, FDA has concluded that this is not the case for cannabidiol."

Brandon explains: "The FDA says GW Pharmaceuticals was carrying out a substantial investigation for CBD as a drug before it was marketed as a dietary supplement. For it to not be permissible as a dietary supplement, there had to be thorough investigations that were made public. It looks like that never actually happened until late 2013, after Bluebird and a few other companies were already selling CBD as a dietary supplement nationwide. So according to the Dietary Supplement Health and Education Act (DSHEA) of 1994, we think CBD should be grandfathered in because we believe that it was already on the market prior."

Not knowing how the issue will ultimately resolve, Brandon says Bluebird is undergoing an overhaul. "Just in case the FDA is correct that GW was carrying out substantial investigations before we were selling it, we have changed our marketing. We no longer sell CBD products; instead, we market full spectrum hemp extracts that contain all the cannabinoids. There are over 80 different naturally occurring cannabinoids in hemp. CBD happens to be in there, but we won't be marketing the CBD as a stand-alone product. Cannabis oil and hemp extracts have been marketed as food and as ingestible items for thousands of years around the world and more than one hundred years in US literature, dating far before any clinical drug investigations about them. That was a way for us to completely remove ourselves from this CBD-dietary supplement issue."

Should the FDA change its position, Brandon says Bluebird can always go back to selling CBD as a stand-alone product again but admits it's frustrating. "It is a sacrifice because we have a really strong internet presence. If you are to search CBD oil or cannabidiol or wholesale CBD, we're going to come up number one or number two on all those Google searches. We're going to have to sacrifice our SEO and strike CBD from everywhere on the website and all other marketing materials. We won't have as much of an internet presence, but we're willing to do that so long as we have a sustainable strategy."

Considering the economic upside of hemp, Brandon says once most people become informed, they see the value of industrial hemp. "I believe it is a no-brainer for most people," he says. "I think the people that are anti-hemp are either unaware of its importance or whose industries would be negatively impacted, such as the oil and fracking industry, the coal industry, the wood industry—all of those could be nearly fully replaced with hemp. We can make totally sustainable bio-fuel. We could be making, very cheaply, hemp plastics that are completely non-toxic and are 100 percent biodegraded into the earth within 40 days. There are an estimated 50,000 uses for industrial hemp."

Brandon says eventually, hemp will win out. "It's already a multi-billion-dollar industry. Once we pass the Industrial Hemp Farming Act or something similar, or better yet S.2237, the floodgates will open. I've read in multiple reports that the cannabis industry is currently the fastest growing industry in America, and that's without full-fledged legalization. Right now, America is importing more than $500 million worth of industrial hemp products a year, and if we pass the Industrial Hemp Farming Act, that will all be brought home. Our American farmers will have a new cash crop.

"Cannabis is not going anywhere. There is so much potential for this industry. And it's still just beginning."

BLUM OAKLAND

With medical marijuana available in almost half the states in the union and the public's relatively rapid embrace of legalizing recreational cannabis, it can seem surreal that just a couple years ago, local business communities treated dispensary owners as outlaws. Not that it deterred cannabis entrepreneurs, like Blum Oakland's Salwa Ibraham; it simply made them craftier. For example, the Blum Oakland moniker came about because of the difficulty dispensaries had just conducting daily business.

"At that time in the industry it was hard to get a bank account," Salwa recalls. "And there were no such things as trademarks or trademark law for us, so our options for protecting ourselves and our business were limited. We had to be creative with our names to have a semblance of being able to protect ourselves. And for purposes of opening up a bank account, words like *collective* or *healing* or *green* couldn't be in it. You'd get flack and get kicked out. So at least with Blum people were intrigued. *Oh, what is that? A retail shop?* And we'd say: *Why yes, we are a boutique.* Bankers bought that."

It was a professional high-wire act Salwa never anticipated for herself when she took a job with the Oakland Fox Theater renovation rehabilitation project, which was intended to entice San Franciscans to Oakland to help gentrify the city, then in dire economic straits.

"It was completely boarded up, shuttered windows, graffiti everywhere—when the sun set you left downtown Oakland," Salwa says. "And when you heard a news story of someone getting shot in downtown Oakland you'd think: *What were they thinking being out at night?*"

In other words, it was a prime area for revitalization, and that led to the development project for the Oakland Fox Theater. The venue had once been a glittering entertainment palace but fell into disrepair and became a haven for the homeless. Opened in October 1928, the 3,200-seat theater was originally named the Oakland and showed movies—especially the then-new talkies—and presented live performances on stage between the films and newsreels. In March 1929, the theater was renamed the Fox Oakland and flourished for several decades.

After years of declining ticket sales, which mirrored the declining neighborhood, the theater closed in 1965. Although the space was occasionally used for special events including Victorian England reenactments, time took its toll. At one point in the '70s, Oakland's Public Works Department was set to purchase the property, demolish the building, and create a parking lot. But that plan fell through, and the building was eventually designated an Oakland City Landmark and listed on the National Register of Historic Places.

In 1996, the Oakland Redevelopment Agency bought the building, and three years later the Friends of the Oakland Fox started the restoration. In 2004, the Oakland Redevelopment Agency received a grant for additional work. When the Oakland mayor—the once and future California governor, Jerry Brown—needed a location for the Oakland School for the Arts, the redevelopment staff suggested placing the school in the retail and office space that wrapped around the Oakland Fox Theatre.

"It was this gorgeous, gorgeous historical theater site," Salwa says. "And the developer I worked for, his vision was to make it a concert venue. Our thought process was: *How do we get people from San Francisco to come to Oakland? We need to have a kick-ass, awesome concert hall and have great shows. And that's how we're going to get the young kids to come to Oakland and spend money.* And so we worked diligently on that project, which had a very complicated financial structure, and I was in charge of doing fundraising."

Salwa had never done fundraising before, so it was feet to the fire, learn as she went.

"That developer was—and is still—a mentor to me. I call him

the original feminist because he always was always so supportive. There I was 21, 22 years old bossing around these 45-, 50-year-old men. And every time I got push back, he told me: *Oh, no. You go tell 'em what to do. You can do it!* It was absolutely empowering, and I learned so much from that."

Salwa's fundraising led her to politicians, local business owners, and the cannabis entrepreneurs running the local pot carts.

In 1996, California had become the first state to legalize medical cannabis through Proposition 215, the Compassionate Use Act. The push for that legislation had its roots in the AIDS epidemic that ravaged the San Francisco gay community in the 1980s. Patients and doctors reported early on that at least anecdotally marijuana helped eased pain in AIDS patients—later empirically backed up in a study by University of California San Francisco researcher Donald Abrams—which prompted a movement to give the sick and dying access to marijuana. That movement resulted in Prop 215.

"Once it passed, you had an influx of activists that were coming to San Francisco wanting to be part of this movement but guess what? San Francisco's real estate was so expensive they couldn't afford to be there," Salwa explains. "Everyone said: *Well, we can't afford San Francisco; we'll go to Oakland!* So they started picking up the real estate around the theater and began selling medical marijuana. People would come from everywhere and hop from pot shop to pot shop."

The area became known as Old Oaksterdam, a portmanteau of *Oakland* and *Amsterdam*, and city officials realized they needed to regulate their city's fast-growing cannabis business.

"So Oakland created the first dispensary permitting process during that time," Salwa says. "And to this day, the language that Oakland used has been cookie-cuttered around the country in Florida, Maine, New York—you name it. Through fundraising, I was making friends with all of these cannabis dispensaries, and they were so generous. Oaksterdam University and the pot clubs associated with Oaksterdam became the second largest private donor to the project behind Bank of America."

Today, the Oaksterdam neighborhood is revitalized with restaurants, bars, shops, and new apartment buildings, which Salwa says all sprang from turning the Oakland Fox into a concert venue. "And we couldn't have done it without the cannabis industry's support."

Once the theater was up and running, Salwa was ready for a break. "That was way too much stress," she laughs. "By then I was in my mid-20s, and I wanted to do something totally different, something more relaxing."

She got a job with SK Seymour, the parent company of the infamous Oaksterdam University, the first cannabis college in the United States. Founded by activist Richard Lee, the university sought to legitimize the cannabis industry—canna-business—with a curriculum that included horticulture, legal issues, politics, history, civics, economics, extracts, topical applications, business management, dispensary management, and cooking with cannabis. The university campus included the Blue Sky Coffee Shop dispensary, a glass blowing shop, a gift shop, a student union, and a clothing store.

"The idea was to generate foot traffic," Salwa explains, "which was very symbiotic with the idea of the theater and bringing people to the area. So I was working in the parent company and helped oversee a little bit of all the different companies. After I'd been there for about a year, Richard decided he wanted to legalize weed in California. So he self-funded Proposition 19, which was our first effort to legalize recreational cannabis in the state."

Salwa worked for Lee on the Proposition 19 campaign, which lost by a slim margin. "But it was a great learning experience," she says.

Ironically, shortly after the Prop 19 setback, Oakland officials had announced they would issue four more dispensary permits.

"Getting a permit was a competitive process," Salwa says. "It was interesting because at that particular time we had a business Who's Who in Oakland. The Seagram family and several big-money entrepreneurs were sniffing around trying to get one of the dispensary licenses here."

She decided to apply for a license. "I was already involved in the industry, I was familiar and involved in the local politics, so even though I was only about 26 at the time, I felt like I was a good candidate to have my own dispensary. I thought: *I really want to do this. I am going to do this*—I was young and fearless," she laughs. "So I started looking for financial backing, because then as now you need to show financial wherewithal."

Interviewing potential backers was an exercise in endurance. "I probably ended up interviewing almost thirty people to be my financing. I interviewed people who were like: *You know what? Once you get the license, we'll give you a check, and we never want to see you again.* Most of the people I interviewed were a little more reasonable, but the person I felt the most comfortable with, who was the most reasonable with me, was a gentleman named Derek Peterson. He was in the local scene as well and had a Wall Street background."

Before becoming a cannabis entrepreneur, Derek had worked at Crowell, Weedon & Co., Wachovia Securities, and was a senior vice president at Morgan Stanley Smith Barney. In 2009, after learning that a friend's dispensary was clearing millions annually, he saw an opportunity. "I was a finance guy," he told the *Huffington Post*. "I started looking at the products and services utilized in this industry, the economics behind it, and how I could prosper from a peripheral business."

In May 2010 Peterson launched GrowOp Technology, which provided full-service, mobile, hydroponic trailers to grow medical marijuana. Seven months later Morgan Stanley fired him because of his cannabis side enterprise, claiming he had failed to get approval for an outside business activity.

Instead of looking for another job on Wall Street, Derek went all in on cannabis, so when Salwa met him, Derek was eager to be involved with the movement as much as possible. "He ended up becoming my financing, which was great. And we ended up with the number one ranking in the permitting process. We were really proud of that, and it affirmed to us that *Yes, we can do it*. And then we got raided."

Even today, despite snowballing approval by the public, medical cannabis exists in a legal gray area because there is no recognition of medical marijuana under federal law. It remains classified a Schedule I drug, leading agents from the U.S. Marshals Service, Drug Enforcement Agency, and Internal Revenue Service to raid

Oaksterdam University in April 2012, kicking in its doors as well as Lee's personal residence and the Blue Sky Coffee Shop.

"They came in and grabbed everything that they could," Salwa recalls. "They seized all of our computers and all of our equipment and the plants and everything from all of our different shops. And it was a very synchronized effort on their behalf."

Despite the dramatic show of federal force, there was no further legal action. Even so, in the aftermath there was a lot of fear and uncertainty in the California cannabis community. But there was also solidarity and determination. Steve D'Angelo, founder and director of Harborside Health Center, remembers thinking: *This is absolutely outrageous, and I need to get down to Oaksterdam and do something.*

Salwa says none of the agencies involved ever officially stated a reason for the raid. "But I think it was two-fold. Number one was the perception that we used 'drug money' to fund the Prop 19 political campaign, which was about taxing and regulating. And then secondly, because we lost I think they wanted to make an example out of us. We were so public—we were on CNN on a regular basis— that it was just a very quick stab in the heart of the industry. And it worked. Oakland went from having more than three hundred entities interested in those four dispensary licenses to ultimately have only 13 submitting because everyone was scared."

Salwa admits that the raid was a very traumatic event and she was as rattled as everyone else. "It was totally scary, and it took me a while to lick the wounds."

But in the end, the possibility of securing a dispensary license was an opportunity too big to pass up. And she found strength from the community. "I had a couple of activist friends tell me: *You know what? This is your time. Patients need to be served. It doesn't matter what the government is doing. If you're really in this for the patients, you just have to keep going.* So I kept going, and we ended up opening our doors in November 2012."

Currently, Blum Oakland is the second largest dispensary in the city, behind Harborside, which is the largest in the United States. They see at least seven hundred patients a day. Just when it seemed the medical cannabis industry had settled into a relatively stable period, more change is on the horizon. In November 2016, California voters passed Proposition 64, legalizing adult recreational marijuana use. Looking back, Salwa suggests maybe the industry want's ready for legalization the first time around.

"People in the industry didn't understand what recreational would do to us. They were comfortable with the way things were. Everybody knew how they were going to make their money. But if we go recreational, what's going to happen? Everybody wanted to see a different example first, and Colorado became an excellent example of what recreational legalization does to the business. And now that we've seen the numbers from Colorado and then Washington and then Oregon and all of the data that's come out, I think we're all looking forward to embracing it."

But even before the winds of acceptance started to blow, Salwa says, "I ended up going a different route because I had a business partner who had a company on the pink sheets, and he was able to uplist to the OTCQX."

For the investment challenged, Investopedia defines *pink sheets* are daily publications compiled by the National Quotation Bureau with bid and ask prices of over-the-counter (OTC) stocks. Unlike companies on a stock exchange, companies on the pink sheets system do not need to meet minimum requirements or file with the Security and Exchange Commission. Pink sheets can also refer to OTC trading. The OTC Markets Group, or OTCQX, is a New York-based financial market providing price and liquidity information for around 10,000 over-the-counter securities.

Translation: Salwa wanted to go public. "And so in 2016, we became the first dispensary to uplist to the OCTQX, and we are currently publicly traded [under the name CareTech], which is exciting for us, and it is exciting for the industry. We have 37,000 shareholders that are all invested in our cannabis dispensary, and they're all rooting for us. They all want us to expand. It's a way for someone in Wyoming to be part of the industry. And you can see from the forums—man, they are an active group," she laughs.

Salwa has now established a fully vertically integrated system. "I grew it from a dispensary to a dispensary and cultivation, and then from that to also an extraction facility. And then while we were getting that up and running, I became senior vice president of CareTech for their cannabis division and expanded our licensing footprint in Nevada. So by the end of 2016, we'll have three dispensaries in Las Vegas and one in Reno; we'll have two cultivation centers in Reno and Vegas; and two production facilities in Reno and Vegas. Our goal is to expand Blum and Blum's name to make it … I don't want to say the Starbucks of cannabis dispensaries, but there is something to be said about being a recognizable brand.

"If you go to the Blum in Oakland, when you're on vacation in Vegas, you'll go to that dispensary and see the same products that you know and are familiar with, along with a similar store layout and feel. So wherever you go, you'll have the same sort of experience that you've come to expect."

While there is excitement among California's cannabis players for a legal recreational market, there's also a circle-the-wagons attitude against outsiders from making a land grab to profit at the expense of the established community. "For folks who've been in the industry a long time, we just want to make sure that our footprint is held, that our roots are deep, and that we expand. I'd be lying if I didn't admit there's a little bit of nervousness about competing against the big boys. You've got these huge capital investment firms coming in that are either looking to buy up a bunch of dispensaries, or they're just looking at coming in and possibly undercutting a lot of the dispensaries, so they have to fold. There's a lot that can go on."

That concern aside, Salwa believes the sheer economic potential of cannabis is changing political attitudes. "I think that once they track the dollars with the states, it's going to be an astonishing number. Cannabis has become an issue that is discussed and is no longer taboo to talk about as a political debate. It's been reported that government agencies are increasing production of cannabis for DEA-registered researchers. There have also been reports of attempts to solve the banking-related issues, another sign of progress."

Beyond the politics, Salwa observes that the mainstreaming of cannabis has sparked a national curiosity of its potential. "The more education that people have regarding the subject, the more likely we can pass progressive laws and dispel myths," she says. At her most hopeful, Salwa can envision federal legalization within a matter of years, not decades, although she concedes, "Even then, I think we will see that some areas will not be as receptive, similar to how some places still have wet and dry counties for alcohol. But as more and more research and data surrounding the negative effects of prohibition is released, it will be difficult to argue against legalization."

And the passage of Proposition 64 may well be the tipping point. The state that started the medical marijuana revolution may well do the same for recreational and even industrial hemp. Salwa notes, "If California, the eighth largest economy in the world, can demonstrate sensible policy that allows for full legalization, we can change the course of the cannabis movement for the country. And the world."

CANNALINE PACKAGING

Despite the increasing acceptance of medical and recreational marijuana, it will take a while for the cannabis industry to emerge from the shadows of nearly a century of political demonization. While the lion's share of entrepreneurial attention focuses on cultivation, edibles, and dispensaries, some forward-thinking businessmen like Arnold Heckman and Andy Rickert are identifying huge opportunities in ancillary products and services.

In 2009 Arnold and Andy started Cannaline, which offered a variety of packaging options for cannabis products. Their journey from mainstream corporate America to the cannabis industry—which still prides itself on its renegade and guerilla roots—was informed and driven by left brain business savvy and right brain creative expression.

Throughout his career, Arnold has been involved in a number of industries. He began in home furnishings, which he describes as "somewhat of a fashion industry. I went to work for a Virginia manufacturer and ended up opening a chain of high-end furniture stores for them in Houston, Texas, when the city was booming."

Arnold spent three years in Texas until a fire at the furniture factory led to the stores closing. "My wife and I came back to Maryland and opened Corporate Investment, a business and commercial real estate brokerage firm." He says the model was similar to a real estate brokerage, "but a lot more complicated. We were a boutique mergers-and-acquisitions firm for smaller businesses. Our sweet spot was in the $250,000 to $10 million range. And we did that for more than 30 years."

At the company's peak, Arnold had more than a sixteen brokers working for him, and the company closed nearly 1,500 transactions. And then came the Great Recession in 2008. "The economy made that a very challenging business. You just couldn't get anything financed," he recalls. "Fortuitously, I had a friend, Steve DeAngelo, who had opened Harborside Health Center—currently the largest dispensary on the planet—in Oakland, California. He's from the DC area, and on one of his visits back we got together for lunch."

They talked about the cannabis industry, and Arnold posed the question that would set him on a new career path. "I asked him what some of the challenges were, and he said one of them was getting quality packaging." The primary purpose of packaging is to keep the medicine fresh, but at the same time it would ideally also provide added perceived value and promote the dispensary's brand. "Steve was having a difficult time getting any packaging companies to take him seriously. Back in 2007, the fact that it was a cannabis-related business meant people didn't understand it or want much to do with it," Arnold chuckles.

Even though medical marijuana had been legal in California since 1996, it was still outside the mainstream business establishment. "It didn't have the exposure that it has now," Arnold notes. "And nobody understood the business or what he needed. So I said: *Steve, it seems fairly simple to me. At the quantities you are using, you should be able to go off-shore and have them custom made to your specifications, and bring them in.*"

Steve said in a later interview that initially, Harborside was using "polyethylene baggies for our grams and a higher grade plastic bag for larger sizes, although we were stuck with stock sizes that were often a compromise, and we had to hand-apply the labels."

The dispensary also used glass jars for their top-shelf offerings. Glass was, and still is, considered the gold standard for cannabis packaging. They ordered from a candle jar company, but the jars would often arrive broken, the lids didn't fit well, and they didn't have a particularly good seal. They'd use what they could and hand-apply labels.

Arnold says he told Steve: *"There's has to be somebody in California with import-export connections. They should be able just to source it for you, and bring it in for you.* To me, it seemed pretty simple. So Steve looked at me. *Arnold, why don't you go have them made, and I'll buy them from you."*

Steve didn't have to ask twice. Arnold reached out to Andy Rickert, a business acquaintance he knew from his Corporate Investment days who was already in the import/export business. Andy owns skinconsultation.com that produces high-end skincare products in the US but imports its packaging through a contact in Asia, giving Andy the experience Arnold knew the new company would need.

So, when the opportunity with Steve presented itself, Arnold told Andy: *I've got an interesting opportunity for us, if you're interested* and told him what it was.

Andy admits he was more than a little surprised. "Honestly, I was shocked because I was very much brainwashed like a lot of people are—not just in this country, but throughout the world. At the time I thought that cannabis was like cocaine, heroin, and LSD. So when Arnold asked me, I was like: *Are you kidding me?* But then he gave me the education I should have had a long time ago; the education everybody should have."

Once fully informed through Arnold's input and his own research, Andy's perspective did a 180, and he agreed they had a golden opportunity to fill a much-needed niche. "I had acquired a skincare company back in 2003, and it taught me that packaging is critical," Andy says. "Look at Estée Lauder; it's the packaging that sells more than the product itself. Some entrepreneurs get it; some don't."

Andy notes how at the beginning of legalized medical cannabis, not all of it was good. But now nearly everyone knows how to grow it properly, so the difference between the best and the average keeps getting smaller and smaller, which makes packaging even more critical to getting noticed and establishing your brand.

Arnold laughs remembering how he went from suit and tie to blue jeans and T-shirts working in Andy's basement. "Now, it was a nice basement. He had a fairly big house, so we had adequate room. We installed an IP phone system, and we had computers, and we had Skype, and we just started working."

Arnold and Andy collaborated closely with Harborside to determine what product designs would best meet the dispensary's needs. "For one, they needed glass jars that actually fit together," Arnold says. "They would get jars where the bases came in one box and the lids in another, and it was just fraught with problems."

Also, after doing an analysis of the cost of buying labels and the labor to put them on, they determined that for the same price, they could fuse decals that would never come off onto the glass jars, which provided a far superior product.

"So we ordered the glass jars and, of course, I thought it would be very simple," Arnold says. "I quickly found out that when it comes to manufacturing, nothing's simple. We had our growing pains trying to get things dialed in; that's an ongoing issue with overseas manufacturing. But I'm happy to say that at this point we've got it under control. Now we are big customers to our factories, so they pay much more attention to quality control than they typically would for smaller customers."

Andy says that when he and Arnold started Cannaline, they thought an initial investment of about $100K would be enough money to reach a breakeven point. It ended up taking several hundred thousand. "That was due in part to the rapid demand for our products, which forced us to buy and stock more and more inventory," Andy explains.

It's a bit ironic that Cannaline outsources because the cannabis industry has a long tradition of supporting local communities. But Arnold says it was both a logistics and cost issue. "I initially tried to source in the US and talked to several manufacturers, one of which told me their minimum order quantity was one million units, and that they would not do any decorating on the jars. To get that done I'd have to ship them to another company, and then ship them again to my warehouse. And then they told me the custom molds for what I wanted would be $75,000. We produced the same molds in Asia for a fraction of that and had the ability to manufacture custom items in much lower quantities."

Cannaline started with jars and then looked for a container suitable for concentrates. "The only thing available was a small, plastic, cube-shaped box that was affectionately known as a *cubie*," Arnold says. "But they were very expensive—upwards of 50 cents each—and they didn't have a good seal because it was just a friction fit. We looked at that and thought there had to be a better way."

The first criterion was shape. Arnold wanted it round, so there were no corners for the concentrate to get stuck in; second, it needed a lid that screwed on, so it didn't come open in a user's pocket. Cannaline developed a custom mold for a small concentrate container, and they were able to retail it for 15 cents. "That was a big hit," Arnold says. "And that design led to other units made of acrylic and then silicone. Now, we have one in glass."

Arnold says building a client base happened organically. It was mostly word of mouth and the Internet. "One of the smarter things we did was to concentrate on optimizing our website. At the time, there were no dedicated cannabis packaging companies, so it didn't take long before we were on the first page of Google when you searched for *marijuana* or *cannabis packaging*. We never paid a penny for pay-per-click. That web optimization allowed people to find us, and unlike many web-based companies, we wanted people to call us. That's what we're all about. Our whole business model was designed to find out what our customers needed and then to create a cost-effective solution."

They quickly outgrew Andy's basement, and the executive offices are now in a three-thousand-square-foot facility, with an additional distribution center on the west coast. But their strategy remains the same: commitment to customer service and being more innovative than the competition.

"Since the beginning, a lot of what we've done has been to custom develop products that nobody had," Arnold says. "Of course, I normally only get a six-month jump before other companies just copy them," he sighs, adding that product development is now his primary focus. "It's an ongoing process that never stops. I've got some interesting and revolutionary new packaging ideas in the pipeline right now."

Cannaline continues to have close professional ties to Asia. Andy says they maintain a warehouse there, which enables them to check products for quality and provides a place to stage their inventory before shipping. "It's expensive to ship," Andy notes, "so we ship in

40-foot containers on a regular basis. That's one of the ways we keep the cost down because even though we believe we have the best quality, we still have to be competitively priced."

Arnold adds: "Our associate in Asia is a great resource for us. I work with him almost daily on product development, and he has many connections there with manufacturing companies. He checks out the manufacturers, ensures quality control, and works with them to produce products based on our specifications."

Arnold says they have investigated the possibility of making some products using hemp polymers, "but the technology is not quite there yet," he reports. "A lot of people advertise that they have hemp plastic, but they don't. It's just not cost-effective, so nobody's doing it to any degree—yet. This industry is very quality-conscious, but also very cost-conscious. So you're always balancing that. I've had a lot of people say they'd love to get plastic bags made out of hemp, or a biodegradable material, and we want to supply them, but we're not quite there yet as far as affordability and technology. We could do it now, but it's going to feel like a potato chip bag and cost two or three times more. Once they hear that they say: *No, that's okay. Your current bags are fine,*" he laughs.

Until industrial hemp is established, Cannaline will continue to utilize existing materials in innovative ways such as the flexible packaging for the smell-proof bags. Arnold admits, "Making a bag as smell-proof as possible—and at the same time have it seal well and keep the product fresh—was a technical challenge due to the nature of cannabis. But smell-proof bags were, and are, a big driver of the growth of the business."

But with success comes competition, which has been increasing in recent years. "Our niche has been the ability to supply great quality products and custom-print them at no additional charge. We were promoting that six years ago, and it was one of the things that Harborside was very big on. They wanted to logo everything that went out the door because cannabis is an agricultural product with no intrinsic brand. It analogous to a plain banana that once branded becomes a Chiquita banana."

Steve agrees. "Never underestimate the importance of branding. As our industry matures the dispensaries that thrive will be the ones that understand the importance of branding and that promote their brand at every opportunity."

Arnold says that message is clearly getting through. "Now everybody is starting to realize that you have to brand your cannabis products. They've really jumped onto the bandwagon, so not only do we have a good selection of stock solutions that people will put labels on, but we also do a significant volume of custom-printed packaging solutions."

Aware that many startups are cash strapped, Arnold argues their services offer a tremendous value. "The minimum order quantities are not that high if you're doing a reasonable amount of the business, and it's considerably more cost-effective than hand applying labels. We can provide a custom-printed bag for the same price as a plain bag. When the bags are manufactured, whether you print them or not, the material's the same. Our additional cost is in making the printing plates, but if you order a reasonable quantity, we will absorb that cost. We have developed a real niche for that, one that people have tried to copy.

"But so far, from what we can see, those competitors have not had the kind of success we have because it's hard. You need a technically-adept factory, technically-adept designers, and you have to have strong quality control to make sure they are produced to specifications. If our customer is not happy, we're going to make them again. That's the arrangement we have with our factories: if they don't come out right, they have to be remade. We've built the business on customer satisfaction and have picked up a lot of business because people have been unhappy with the custom printed packaging from some of our competitors."

Andy adds: "When we started, we had a friend who did the custom design work we needed. But at the end of 2013, we had so much work we hired a professional designer. He's a graduate from a top design school and knows both the artistic, creative, and technical aspects needed to create great designs. Then, in the middle of 2016, we hired a second designer, as it was clear that there were not enough hours in the day for one designer to keep up with the demand. Now we have two full-time, high-end, professional designers to work on customer requests for custom packaging."

Arnold says, "As the cannabis industry matures, it's becoming more professional as entrepreneurs start adopting basic business principles and marketing strategies, along with the realization that professionally designed packaging can be a critical component to their success. We introduced the importance of having quality packaging. When we came into the industry, almost everyone was using cheap poly bags."

Arnold admits it has sometimes been an uphill battle convincing small dispensary owners and start-ups on the value of custom packaging. "I often say that you can put a Tiffany ring in a K-Mart box, or a K-Mart ring in the Tiffany box, and people will take the Tiffany box every time. You can have the best product in the world, but if no one looks at it, it will never sell."

With every state that legalizes cannabis, Cannaline's pool of potential customers grows—as does their competition—so remaining the packaging leader becomes more challenging with each passing year.

"Everyone who comes into the market has one proven way to penetrate the market, and that's to sell cheaper," Arnold notes. "We started the same way. We looked at this market and believed we could sell a better product for less than what was then available. And that's what we did by manufacturing in large quantities, which we still do, and passing those savings on to our customers. Now I see some companies offering similar-sized bags—but not necessarily the same quality—for a penny less than ours. Undercutting us on quality—and therefore price—is the only way they're going to get the business. We could make that same bag for two cents less but have no intention of compromising our reputation by providing a lower quality product."

Arnold says he knows he'll lose some clients who only consider cost as opposed to value. "Look, I could make products cheaper than anybody, if I was willing to compromise the quality. When I design products I never say to my factories: *I want a product that's going to cost X* because then my factories will try to figure out a way to do that by cutting corners. Instead, I say: *Here's what I want. I want it top quality. I want it to be the best it can be for what we're trying to do. How much is it going to cost?* Sometimes the price point doesn't work for us, but most times, in the quantities we order, it does. I want our factories to make money. I want Cannaline to be important to them."

In general, it comes down to a quantity issue. "If I order 30,000 the price is X; if I order 250,000, it might be 30 percent less. Some small businesses can't afford the mold cost for custom products or the inventory necessary to get the best prices. If we think the product is ultimately going to sell millions of units, we'll absorb the cost of the mold and order in large quantities to bring the overall cost down."

The same philosophy drives the design process. "If I see a flaw in the design, that means the factory has to make a new mold. In the end, it costs us a little more but results in a superior product. By designing this way, I tend to get a top-quality product because I'm not forcing the factories to cut corners, which they will do to meet a price. They're used to giving a price and then having the client say they want it for half the price. But then you've got problems all the way down the line because it'll look like what you specified, but it won't be what you specified. So our approach is different. Our attitude is: *Let's just do it without compromise, and make a better product.* And we've built the business on delivering a no-compromise product," Andy says, by following the philosophy that "every client is our most important client."

Although they anticipate the company will continue to grow, in the end, Arnold and Andy are more concerned with quality than quantity. "I have no illusions about necessarily being the biggest," Arnold says. "I just want Cannaline to be the best. We're never going to be the Walmart of packaging. That's not what we're about. We want to provide exceptional customer service with the highest-quality products at a fair price. As long as we continue to do that, the rest will take care of itself."

FOREVER FLOWERING GREENHOUSES

While the apple may not fall far from the tree, in Jonathan Valdman's case, it's more the flower doesn't fall far from the cannabis plant. "I'm a second-generation cannabis grower and smoker," he says. "My parents both smoked and had a couple of plants in the backyard. I've been growing cannabis for about 23 years, long before it was legal. In one way or another, my entire life has been supported by cannabis."

Raised in Southern California, Jonathan eventually migrated north. In 1996 when California voters passed Prop 215 legalizing the use of medical marijuana, he started growing cannabis legally. His commitment to sustainability is what spurred his interest in greenhouses.

"I was living in Mendocino County at the time, and everybody I knew in the area was growing organically, wearing hemp, eating organically, driving bio-diesel—really living this alternative lifestyle and growing cannabis for a living," he explains. "But a lot of people had a barn full of grow lights, and I didn't see that closing the loop on a sustainable approach to life that we were all embarked on living."

At the time, Jonathan had already been experimenting with growing techniques. "I saw that a yearly paycheck of just growing one crop under the sun was not necessarily the most dependable way to move forward. That led me [to believe] that light deprivation was the direction this industry was headed because you have the quantity and the efficiency of sun grown, but the quality and the control of indoor lamp grown."

Light deprivation (light dep), is the ability to control how many hours of light a plant receives. When cannabis growing was illegal, the plants were typically grown indoors under grow lights. Light dep was controlled by simply turning the lights on and off. In a greenhouse, blackout fabrics are used to control the light.

The main difference between growing indoors and outdoors is the amount of energy the grower uses. Jonathan says it was clear that growing indoors was not a sustainable business model once growing cannabis became legal. "So many people were going to start growing that the exponential amount of energy they would consume was going to be an environmental travesty."

In 2006 Jonathan established Forever Flowering

Greenhouses (FFG) with a focus on reducing the carbon footprint of cannabis production. FFG became the first greenhouse company to focus solely on cannabis production. Jonathan fervently believes that cannabis is more than just a cash crop; he views it as an avenue for social change. "Once we start focusing on hemp with the textile and fuel industries, and in nutrition and biofuels, that's when we're going to see a revolution occur, because there is not much that cannabis can't do. You can even make plastic out of hemp-based polymers."

But he acknowledges that the public needs to be educated on hemp's value because traditionally the only focus was on recreational cannabis as opposed to industrial hemp.

"There are very few questions that face us as a society that cannabis is either not the answer to or not part of the answer to. Until now, people focused on the THC aspect of cannabis, and that has been a multi-billion dollar underground existing industry here in California for about fifty years. Now nationwide we see it as a multi-billion-dollar industry."

He notes how five years ago few people had heard of cannabidiol (CBD). "Now, thanks to people like Dr. Sanjay Gupta, the vast majority of people that have any understanding whatsoever of cannabis know what CBD is and know what the medicinal and health aspects of it are. And one of the reasons why we know about this is because laws are finally starting to loosen up so that we're able to have funding to do research."

For the past five thousand years, Jonathan notes, people merely had personal, anecdotal experiences with cannabis' health benefits. "Now we have the ability to do real lab testing and lab research. It's opening up this whole new world that didn't necessarily exist before. We have no idea what the new miracle cure, the new miracle application of cannabis will be this year, next year, or 10 years from now. I mean, Ford created his first vehicle all with hemp polymers. So it's not a question of: *Can it be done?* It's: *Why was it stopped being used?* And that opens a whole wormhole. Hemp can replace anything made out of plastic, but it is in Big Oil's interest to keep things on an oil-based economy."

Jonathan believes the hemp plant's versatility—its nutritive aspects, building material aspects, polymer aspects, medicinal aspect, and for many its spiritual aspect—makes it perhaps the most valuable plant on earth. "There are so many different ways that cannabis can address all these different issues. That's why we hear so many people say how hemp is the healing of the nation or how hemp can save the planet. There is very little that hemp cannot be applied to."

Jonathan's commitment to sustainability also led him to embrace permaculture, which stands for permanent agriculture. The term was coined in the late 1970s and represents the sustainable alternative to traditional agriculture. In an interview with *Mg*, Jonathan noted, "Conventional agriculture tends to degrade the planet by monocropping the same crops over and over until they lose layers of topsoil. Permaculture is regenerative and allows you to bring land back to life and create food forests and systems where, for instance, the roof of your house catches rainwater that's then put back into your garden. It creates systems consistent with a living landscape. It's more than being sustainable—which has become as overused a word as *organic* at this point. It means that we're trying not to do any worse than how we're doing right now, that we'll be able just to coast along right where we are."

The idea behind regeneration, he explains, is to take areas and make them better than how the farmer found them. "That's a huge thing that I see cannabis making possible because in the form of hemp it is actually regenerative to the earth. I was talking to these folks who are looking at a project in South Africa in which they will grow hemp and from that hemp make lumber, and then use that lumber to rebuild towns and villages that have been crumbling since apartheid, regenerating not only the planet but actual communities and civilizations."

In the end, once consumers learn about hemp and its inherent regenerative properties, Jonathan believes government policies will follow suit. But educating the public is just one of numerous responsibilities of the cannabis industry as a whole.

"I see the current industry as a circle within a larger circle. The cannabis industry is the large circle and within that the smaller circle is the cannabis community. It is the responsibility of those of us from the community to educate the people that are just getting into the industry as to the heritage and culture of this plant and the people and communities around it and the possibilities that are inherent when working within its sphere of influence." Getting involved in local and national political levels is the kind of direct grassroots effort needed to enable the industry to achieve its potential. Jonathan's home of Nevada County, California, has recently been part of a David and Goliath story of voting down an imposed ban on outdoor cultivation, an unprecedented and miraculous victory for their small, mountain community. Jonathan says stakeholders must become active participants in local politics to help pass cannabis-friendly regulation just as they did in Nevada County.

The journey from illegal grower to legit cannabis entrepreneur to hemp industry visionary to social and political advocate has sometimes seemed surreal. "I definitely had the realization that I traded in my pick and my shovel for a laptop and a cell phone," Jonathan laughs. "Everybody says that on the black market side of things everything's a hustle, if you will. But what I've found is that running a legitimate business is the real hustle. Your margins are a lot slimmer, you've got a lot more competition that is in your face, and you're a lot more transparent, so you're also a lot more vulnerable."

In addition to now paying taxes, legalization also means having to be in compliance with the myriad of local, state, and federal regulations of running a business. The complexity facing growers prompted Jonathan to co-found The Cannabis Conservancy (TCC), which is a third-party certification for sustainability and best management practices in the cannabis industry. TCC's certification helps create resiliency for cannabis farmers by creating a relationship between the consumer and the people that produce the products they are choosing to purchase via a QR code program titled MYGrow.

Recognizing and rewarding the farmer for their beyond-organic practices helps to build their brand and create consumer loyalty. Along with assurance of best practices and upstanding company values, the certification also creates consumer safety by requiring that all products be lab tested for pesticides and any other processes that may be harmful for human consumption.

"The way we assist farmers or startups in creating or bettering their internal organization is to have them become compliant with our standards and providing them with templates of how to create a quality management system (QMS) as well as having updated standard operating procedures (SOP) in place. That helps a farmer to look at their business practices and structure their company in a way that investors will now find attractive as well," Jonathan explains, adding, "It's a bit daunting right now in California, which differs from other states. The majority of the nation is creating laws and then creating a cannabis industry around those laws. But here in California, we have an established cannabis industry that we now have to create regulations around it to fit this existing system."

His success as an entrepreneur has not dulled his personal efforts to follow a sustainable lifestyle or his commitment to his local community. "It's what I base the majority of my decisions on. We do everything we can, but we can't do everything—purchasing local, supporting my community, and making sure that the money stays where I live as much as possible. I look at the price of something as not being the bottom line in my decision-making process."

He explains that people often lose sight of the hidden costs of low prices. "When we're supporting cheap equipment, or cheap material, or cheap food, or cheap medicine, what does it mean when you look at a grander picture of things? Cheap equipment will have to be maintained and replaced more often costing money and filling up landfills. If you're eating cheap food, well, where is that being grown? How is it being transported to here? What is the environmental impact of bringing South American-grown produce into California or Washington or wherever it is? You start looking at what the herbicides and pesticides are doing to the areas that it is being produced in and applied to. And what is happening to us when we consume this food grown with pesticides that isn't providing the nutrition we need? This cheap, imported food is now making us sick, and we need to include the medical bills that go to treating diseased bodies that are malnourished and fed with faux food. So, I really try to look at the whole perspective when making decisions."

FFG, which began as a local startup, has now evolved into an international business and Jonathan credits his general manager Eric Brandstad as being an integral part of the company's growth and continued success. Eric says he didn't set out to be a management guy; he was a freelance grading contractor who did some site development for FFG in its early days.

"I went over to see them putting the first greenhouse together, and I felt like it wasn't the best job of grading," Eric recalls. "So I jumped on the builder's tractor and ended up doing the work the builder said they couldn't do."

After the impromptu demonstration of his expertise, Eric told the builder, "Okay, look … it appears to me you guys need someone to come in and do the site prep. I'll do that, and then you guys come in and do the build."

That arrangement lasted two years until around 2008, "when the economy tanked, and even cannabis growers were watching their budgets, so most of the work dried up," Eric says.

To get more tractor jobs—and keep a roof over his head—Eric became proactive. "I asked Jonathan for a stack of brochures then went out and passed them around to all the people I knew who might be interested. My thought was if I could drum up greenhouse business for Jonathan, in turn it would get me the tractor work."

Eric's efforts led to an unexpected job offer and career change. "Jonathan hired me to help do marketing and sales. So I started answering the phones for Forever Flowering and driving the tractor at the same time. We were trying to get the message out there about light deprivation greenhouses, which were new for most people. Even though a lot of growers knew about the technique, nobody had thought about its commercial viability. It took a lot of years of doing trade shows, advertising, and Jonathan pouring his own money into the company to keep it going. But eventually we started gaining some traction, to the point where I now spend all my time at the office, and at trade shows, and that kind of thing. The company's going like gangbusters, but I do wish I could get back out on the tractor once in a while," he admits with a laugh.

As global interest in sustainability and lowering energy costs increases, FFG has grown both in the number of sales and the size of the greenhouses ordered. Jonathan now employs seven, full-time staff and uses many independent contractors to do the installations.

"It's become a decent-sized business over the last 10 years," Jonathan says, noting he was self-taught and learned by doing. "That's one of the big differences of what we do. We're not a company that saw the green rush, if you will, and then tried to figure out a way to get involved. We were the actual people doing it and figuring out: *How do we create a business out of this?*" he laughs. "I saw a need and created a product. Then I created the market and social tribe around that product and then built a company to serve those aspects."

Eric says FFG is based on "building a good rapport with people and not draining everybody's pockets. We try to help people with their budgets and concerns and maybe even their ability levels to get what they need so that they can either learn or scale up and be successful. I spend a lot of time educating, which has translated into making sales."

Jonathan adds, "All the education that we give freely, everything we do, all the products that we sell, is all based on our personal experience, research, and development. One of the things that separate us as well is that we have the ability to tell you why we do the things we do and why we don't do the things we don't do. Very few companies can give you that kind of information. Mostly because they just straight out don't know, so a lot of people are just theorizing that *this should work*, or *that should happen like that*, but very few are basing their company and their product offerings on their personal experience."

Jonathan says for as much as the cannabis industry has grown, been legitimized through legalization, and matured through the efforts of grassroots organizations, his goal is the same as it's always been: to see cannabis reach its full environmental, social, and cultural potential.

"I feel that cannabis has the potential to be the global leader in sustainability, and the first step in that process was creating products that help people produce cannabis in a sustainable manner with a reduced carbon footprint. That's where Forever Flowering came about, and after 10 years I am now reaching out and exploring new possibilities with the Cannabis Conservancy; how do we identify the companies that are growing responsibly, that are going above and beyond, and reward them for what they're doing? Because as a grower, most people know that when you sell your products and it goes on a shelf, nobody knows how it was grown or anything that went into it. Differentiating the products on the shelves and creating a relationship with the farmers that produced it is a brand new concept thanks to regulations that protect people from criminal prosecution."

One of the most exciting developments of the Cannabis Conservancy for Jonathan is the creation of a program called MYGrow where each farmer will get a unique QR code.

"Within that QR code, there will be a template that the farmer can self-populate to tell their story," Jonathan explains. "It gives them a foundation to say who they are, how they cultivate, why they do the things that they do, and what the values of their company are so that they can communicate to the end user what's special about their product and what makes it worth a premium. That, in turn, allows a consumer to go into a dispensary and simply click on a QR code and instantaneously create a relationship with the people that produce the product they are considering buying. They can make an educated choice of what companies they want to support, what products they want to consume, and whose values they align with."

Jonathan believes it will be a turning point because now the market will be able to start driving a company's production aspects.

"Consumers are going to pay a nominal fee for something that was lab tested, created and grown consciously, and has that type of backbone into it, especially when we're talking about the medicinal aspects when people depend on this medicine to do what they've heard it's going to do. And they're trusting that it's clean, they're trusting that it was grown organically. So for the medicinal patient, it's imperative that we implement this right away. And we don't want to turn the recreational user into a medical user because they're consuming products that are not clean."

Jonathan stresses that cannabis is a non-toxic plant. "Nobody has ever died from the direct effects of cannabis use, and nobody has ever become very ill from consuming cannabis. But what we see now is that the methodologies of the way that cannabis is being produced, and the uncleanliness and the tainting of the product with different herbicides or pesticides are what's making people sick. When we take a flower that might have a pesticide residual in the parts per million and then concentrate that and turn it into an oil or an edible., now that part per million is potentially a part per thousand, or a part per hundred, that has become very toxic for human consumption. So, that needs to be looked at and addressed immediately, or we're going to have an industry that's creating a lot of problems. And then it will get over-regulated by federal governments. So, we have to take the responsibility now of how we're cultivating it."

That responsibility includes reducing the energy consumption associated with cannabis that's grown indoors. "The impact that we're having from the energy consumption is truly insane. In the United States right now, they say indoor cannabis production is using more than 1 percent of our national energy consumption. In California, indoor production uses about 9 percent of our energy right now. *And it's not needed*. We can produce the quantity and the quality of cannabis that we need in light deprivation greenhouses year round. And there's no reason why we shouldn't go in that direction."

Jonathan also points out that cannabis is a photosynthesizing plant and as of today there is no bulb on the planet that can replicate the spectrum of the sun leading to reason that indoor cultivation does not allow the plant to reach its full potential.

Plus, he notes, it's also good business. Inside growers will have a hard time competing in an open market. "Why spend all that money on cultivating indoors, when you can just use the sun. And there's the added value of products grown sustainably, grown clean, that are in compliance and certified, and are going above and beyond. Those things over time are going to separate where we are right now, and what the industry is going to look like in the future."

One of the challenges for everyone involved in the rapidly growing cannabis industry is reversing decades of misinformation, scare tactics, persecution, and ignorance. The mission of Max Simon's Green Flower Media is "to change the social stigma of cannabis forever through top quality education and captivating real stories about people who use cannabis. As the nation heads towards legalization, and with 150+ million gen-x and baby boomers looking for better health and wellness options, Green Flower is perfectly positioned to be the go-to source for trusted cannabis education."

Green Flower's content—including online courses for purchase and free articles and downloadable reports—cover 19 topics such as activism, business, DIY, growing, health, how-to, news, science, healthy consumption, and legal rights. And through Simon's skill at combining business savvy, marketing know-how, and a passion for wellness advocacy, Green Flower is now the world's largest e-learning platform for cannabis and hemp education.

Max sees many parallels between the challenges faced by cannabis in gaining public understanding and awareness and the skepticism that greeted the notion of wellness and holistic medicine as represented by Deepak Chopra. He should know. Max says his first big career break after college was landing a job as the Chopra Center's director of consumer products. For the next six years, he rebranded the company and developed dozens of signature products such as supplements, teas, massage oils, and candles; created an optimized e-commerce platform; and established new distribution channels that greatly improved profitability. Max also became an instructor, traveling all over the world to help educate people about mind-body wellness, spirituality, and self-actualization.

He calls it a life-changing experience that filled him with enough confidence to start his own meditation training company for young people. "It was a cool concept, but it was definitely way ahead of its time," Max admits.

A year and a half later he had burned through all of his savings, including an $80,000 inheritance from his grandmother. His startup failed, and after weighing his options, Max focused on what he felt was his strength. So, with his remaining funds, he started Big Vision Business, a new venture designed to help companies maximize their reach through digital marketing, like what he did for Chopra.

The company was a success, but Max didn't feel personally

fulfilled. So along with a partner, he started a streaming service that he describes as Netflix for audiobooks. His partner built the technology while Max focused on acquiring their catalog of more than 15,000 audiobooks and premium training audios. But his involvement would be short-lived.

"I started to have differences with my co-founder," Max says. "Once it became clear we couldn't work it out, I decided to walk away."

For a while Max did come consulting work while waiting to see "what the universe had in store for me next." The answer came when a friend who had a cannabis business needed help promoting his company. Max, who says he's been a cannabis user for years, was intrigued. And the more he learned about the cannabis industry, the more he realized there was a need for his skill set. "I saw a huge hole that I could fill: creating online education for a worldwide audience."

Max established Green Flower Media in 2015 and says there was a sense of déjà vu. "Back when I was at the Chopra Center, meditation, yoga, and alternative therapies were not as widely accepted as they are today. We had something that we knew was genuinely good but at the same time was genuinely stigmatized. Cannabis has the exact problem. You have this plant that I know from both my personal experience and science is a genuinely valuable and good thing to the world. But it's even more stigmatized than [holistic] medicine was back then."

He says the solution he came up with for Chopra was "to broadcast great education and great content in every facet that we could, as many times as we could, to get people to see the truth. So, we started Green Flower to educate people about the truth and the facts and the science of the plant, while also showcasing legitimate experts who could represent the positive side and go against the stigma side."

The acceptance of cannabis in the United States has snowballed over the last decade, first for medical usage and now for recreational. Max thinks there are two main factors at work driving the social sea change.

"First, people are suffering. And the reality is when you're suffering, you look for a solution. And it's almost hard to believe that this one plant can be so effective for so many things, except that it is. That's one reason why the mentality has shifted: no matter how hard they try to impress belief systems, you can't argue with reality. And when somebody who is in pain tries cannabis, and it's more effective at relieving their pain with fewer side effects than prescription drugs, it can't be ignored. Or when somebody who is completely nauseous and unable to eat tries cannabis and can get food down and get healthy, they can't ignore that. Or when a kid who has epilepsy stops having seizures because of CBD oil, you just can't ignore it. And when the science continues to validate that this isn't something that's bad for you, and the plant continues actually to be effective, that's when people's minds change."

Again, Max says the public's evolving perspective mirrors his experience with Chopra. "People can be adamantly against something until they get sick. And at the moment you realize it's better for you to open up to the solution that eases your suffering than it is to remain stubborn."

The second factor facilitating cannabis acceptance is the opportunity cannabis offers. "Let's face it," Max says. "We not only have a desire to alleviate our suffering and our pain, but we also have a desire to achieve. And when you have a brand-new industry being born—literally right before our very eyes—that's generating billions of dollars, people get interested. The more you get interested in something, the more you get educated, and the more you learn. And then you start telling everybody else about it. So I think the combination of this plant relieving suffering, the industry's rapid growth and the excitement that comes from smart people getting educated about how to succeed in it are the reasons why it's tipping so fast."

Max even views setbacks, like the Federal Drug Administration's decision to keep cannabis a Schedule I drug, in a glass half full light. "To me, it just lights a fire underneath us and fuels the depth of our passion for what we do to end the misinformation and the propaganda. I find it really sad on a human level because the deeper I get into cannabis, the more I see that this is a public health issue and a social justice issue. We have millions and millions and millions of people who are suffering very deeply with their health concerns, and this plant can fix them."

He feels the government's stance on cannabis is not in the best interest of the public. "Decisions like that say: *We don't care about the health of our society* or *We are more driven by politics or a political agenda.* And it makes me sad, but it also simply makes us more intensely passionate about what we do because it's all about education. That FDA decision was just because the people making those choices are still misinformed. They're truly being lied to and they're believing it. But again, I have a unique perspective because of my work with Chopra. Yes, it was a different industry and different time, but I've watched things go from being rejected and laughed at to being widely accepted and celebrated. So our mission and our purpose are to educate the world through our online content and our online classes to change that. It just takes some time."

But Max believes we're at the point where it will be sooner rather than later. Since 1996 when California became the first state to legalize medical marijuana, he says the industry has done a lot of work to inform the public. "But over the last few years in particular things are really starting to accelerate. If we look at it through that lens, there's probably another three or five years of this kind of push-pull happening."

He says he has zero doubt that in the not-so-distant future people will wonder what the fuss was all about. "When we were at Chopra, people would be appalled at, and adamantly opposed to, the idea of meditation and yoga benefitting your health. And now here we are today, and mind-body wellness is accepted the world over. It will be the same with cannabis."

On the Green Flower Media website, users can access a library of free reports such as *The Healthiest Ways to Consume Cannabis, The Benefits of Juicing Cannabis vs. Eating Hemp Seeds, What is Super Soil?* and *How to Talk to Your Kids*. The site also offers a variety of video courses. Subjects covered include *Treating Sick Kids with Cannabis: The Truth, the Science, & the Stories; Making Smart Investments into the Cannabis Industry; Secrets of the Most Successful Cannabis Entrepreneurs;* and *Insomnia & Cannabis: A 100 Percent Natural Approach to Restful Sleep*.

The courses range from an hour to multiple parts. For example, *Cannabis as Medicine* is a three-part video series that presents why and how cannabis works to heal so many different physical and mental conditions. One review of the course outlined the content:

> *Cannabis as Medicine* will feature ten of the industry's
> most knowledgeable physicians, activists, and experts . . .

The first video introduces the endocannabinoid system. Each and every one of us—and many animals, for that matter—have an endocannabinoid system that helps to regulate our body's normal functioning. Our bodies naturally make chemicals called endocannabinoids, and when we have a deficiency of endocannabinoids things start to go wrong.

The following two videos will . . . help you understand how the endocannabinoid system functions and why it works for certain medical conditions.

The endocannabinoid system is still very new, only having been discovered in the 90s . . . and there is a lot about this system that has yet to be explored. If you or a loved one is suffering from cancer, chronic pain, insomnia, depression, anxiety, seizures, inflammation, migraines, PTSD, arthritis, Alzheimer's, menstrual cramps, nausea, or asthma among others ailments, this video series will help you understand how cannabis could be the perfect alternative medicine.

"Our business model is based on creating online classes and courses that people can purchase. These are multimedia, classroom type experiences that come with videos and downloads. We also produce a ton of free content that we think is valuable to get out into the world. So, it's a balancing act. But the number of people who buy a course or a class from us on a daily basis allows us to be self-sustaining."

Max estimates Green Flower has had more than 2,500 students already who have paid for classes and materials in addition to the tens of thousands of people who have downloaded the site's free material. He anticipates that at some point, those online visitors will buy classes and courses as well "when something strikes their fancy, or they'll send somebody else to our site that does. But as a business, we can sustain ourselves on that blend of giving out a tremendous amount of good quality free material while also inviting people to pay for some of our premium instruction."

Green Flower is currently focused on adding more material to their library, from general knowledge reports to state-specific legal information. "What we have right now is not nearly the capacity that we will within the next 12 to 24 months. Our vision and where we're going with Green Flower is that we'll produce state-specific content in each of the genres, as well as content in each of the verticals."

Max says there are three different kinds of education. "There's the health side, which is global. Then there's the industry side, which is very state-specific, that goes into managing and developing the industry. And lastly, there's the kind of growing and do-it-yourself product side that by nature is a little more generalized. So, we produce content in all three of those verticals. Where things are going is we'll have content in all different verticals, localized when it makes sense, and global when it makes more sense that way."

For as bullish as Max is on the future of medical and recreational cannabis, he doesn't see industrial hemp following a parallel track. He believes that for better or worse, lawmakers are just not very educated and not very interested.

"Hemp and cannabis tend to be in different categories, so they are viewed differently in the eyes of government policy and the eyes of the industry," he says. "The only way to do industrial hemp is to grow in volume. But the government is still limiting the amount that people can cultivate because they're still treating it like it's the same thing as consumable cannabis. It needs to be addressed as a separate product, but it's always lumped together with marijuana in ways that end up just hurting the progress."

That doesn't mean Max won't try to educate people on the potential of industrial hemp as well as cannabis. But he acknowledges that it's a challenging topic for Americans to address as a society. "Cannabis has a legal ramification, a social justice ramification, a health ramification, and an industrial ramification. When you put all those components in place, it requires a tremendous amount of dialogue and education to get through it all. But the possibilities of what you can do with cannabis are so vast and so legitimately valuable that it's really easy to become passionate about it once you become educated."

Green Flower's education outreach is expanding beyond online content into presenting live events and conferences, which Max says is a natural evolution. "My team, myself included, has a ton of event background experience, so we definitely will move into the event space. We'll pass 100,000 users this year and expect to reach somewhere between 300,000 to 400,000 next year. One of the things about businesses like ours is as we scale up, we'll have a tremendous ability to move into other industries, other brands, and other ways of utilizing that audience."

In January 2016, Green Flower presented the first annual Cannabis Health Summit, a free, two-day online event that featured 20 doctors, scientists, and cannabis leaders. Each speaker made a TED-style presentation of up-to-date cannabis facts, information, and science. Topics included epilepsy, autism, cancer, and cannabis; treating PTSD, anxiety, and depression; better dosing strategies; how different delivery methods work; and the future of medical cannabis.

According to the Green Flower website, the goal of the summit was multi-fold:

> By bringing together the top experts and giving them the ultimate platform to share their knowledge and wisdom with the world, we hope to solve many of the greatest

cannabis challenges we face today.

1) Clearing away the stigma and mystery:

Think about all the people in this world who could benefit immensely from cannabis but are afraid to give it a try simply because of the stigma or lack of credible information. This event will change all of that. If you know somebody who could benefit, invite them to the Summit!

2) Winning over physicians:

Countless physicians, healthcare providers, and alternative practitioners will be in attendance. Think of the impact we could make on our healthcare system if more leaders in the field truly knew the facts and science.

3) Implementing cannabis as a harm reduction agent:

The numbers for this are already in; opiate fatalities are down by nearly 25 percent in states where cannabis is legal. The Summit will push the numbers even further as we fight this devastating epidemic caused by damaging pharmaceuticals.

4) This event will have a major legislative impact:

Legislators from all over the country and in other parts of the world will be invited to tune in. And reform advocates will also be able to use videos later from the Summit in their efforts to lobby for change and to end the costly war on drugs.

5) Lives will be saved:

Our experts have firsthand accounts that cannabis can indeed save people, improve their quality of life, and allow them to focus on being healthy and happy. This virtual Summit will bring that message to millions, a message steeped in fact-based information and packaged in a way that will allow everybody to gain value and a new understanding of this amazing plant.

In addition to branching into special events, Green Flower has launched a monthly subscription that debuted in October 2016. Max jokes, "You could call it the Lynda.com of cannabis. For a very low monthly fee, people have unlimited access to our whole library of online classes to get trained and educated in all of the topics we offer. It's very cool and an extreme value-driven innovation we're doing. We're taking a model that's already widely loved and accepted and successful in another space, and applying some of the mechanics of that to this brand new industry."

When asked what advice he would give people interested in becoming part of the cannabis industry, Max says, "I'd offer the same advice that Steve DeAngelo (founder of Harborside Medical) told our students in the course he did for Green Flower about entering the cannabis industry: find what you're already passionate about and then apply it to cannabis. I thought it was perfect advice because the cannabis industry is filled with everything that you would look for or find in any other industry."

He cites Green Flower Media as a prime example. "What I love and what I'm passionate about is creating educational media. So I applied it to cannabis. If you're a chef, apply that to creating a line of edibles. If you're a designer, apply that to doing design for cannabis businesses. If you're a writer, apply that to writing in the cannabis space. Whatever you are already passionate about, there is a place for that in cannabis."

HARBORSIDE HEALTH CENTER

Steve Jobs, Rosa Parks, Tim Berners-Lee...From computer technology to civil rights to the Worlds Wide Web, every movement needs a face. Someone who represents any evolution that profoundly changes the cultural, social, and political fabric of life as we know it. Someone whose message of change and forward thinking commands attention. Whose vision mobilizes the already converted and changes the hearts and minds of skeptics. In other words, every movement needs a rockstar.

For cannabis, it's Steve DeAngelo.

Steve DeAngelo has spent most of his life as a cannabis activist, advocate, canna-entrepreneur, and educator. Often called the father of legal cannabis industry for his work to reverse decades of demonizing a plant with unique industrial, medical, and wellness potential, DeAngelo has successfully blended activism with capitalism to create what is arguably the first cannabis business empire. He has founded several socially responsible enterprises including the ArcView Group—which introduce investors to the cannabis community—and most notably Harborside Health Center, the largest medical marijuana dispensary in the world that does a reported $30 million annually in sales. To reach and influence even more people, DeAngelo's 2015 book, *The Cannabis Manifesto*, speaks eloquently on how the real danger isn't cannabis.

"Cannabis is not harmful," he asserts, "but prohibition is."

He points out how the war on drugs has led to the unjust imprisonment of men of color, strengthened and enriched violent cartels, and prevented the development of effective treatments for cancer, epilepsy, and Alzheimer's. He asserts that when marijuana is legal, crime goes down, suicide rates fall, tax revenues rise, and there is an overall increase in wellness. In short, the pros far outweigh any cons.

DeAngelo has said he knows more about cannabis that anyone. Hyperbole aside, he may know more about cannabis activism than anyone because he's been doing it for most of his life. Born in Philadelphia in 1958, he was raised in Washington DC, where his father worked for the Kennedy administration. Steve was exposed to social consciousness as a child through his parents' work as Civil Rights activists and his experiences overseas during his father's two-year stint working for the Peace Corps in India between 1967 and 1969.

When the DeAngelos returned to the United States, the Cultural Revolution was in full swing, and the conflict in Viet Nam was a flash point. Steve started skipping school to attend antiwar demonstrations. In seventh grade he organized a group of students to commandeer the school's gym in a show of solidarity with an antiwar demonstration taking place.

But the elder DeAngelos's social activism didn't include drugs. When he was 13, Steve's parents caught him smoking pot and took his stash. He rebelled by running away from home for a few weeks. Over the next few years, he was kicked out of school on two occasions for his cannabis use and police arrested him for smoking weed in a public park.

When he was 16, Steve dropped out of school to join the Youth International Party, a radical, youth-oriented political movement known for its theatrical protest events. Members of the group called themselves Yippies. Steve was the primary organizer of the annual Fourth of July marijuana smoke-ins in front of the White House.

But as he matured, Steve began to question whether any one party—including his own—had all the answers. "The Yippies theoretically were supposed to be an anarchist, nonauthoritarian group, but within the organization there was a whole system of hidden power and economic structures. So, I learned it was very important to be suspicious of the idea that there could be

91

a revolution that was going to solve all our problems all at once. I learned to be very suspicious of ideology and dogma and political leadership."

While activism might have fed his soul, Steve fed his stomach through various entrepreneurial pursuits. He channeled lessons from his street activism into promotable skills such as event planning, stage management, and promotions that gained him entrée into the music industry. Steve worked as a concert promoter, nightclub manager, and record producer. He renovated and converted two movie theaters into live music venues.

Steve eventually went back to school and graduated summa cum laude from the University of Maryland in 1984. He then opened the Nuthouse, a nine-bedroom home he turned into a sanctuary and gathering spot for Washington, DC-area cannabis activists like Jack Herer, who showed Steve his manuscript of *The Emperor Wears No Clothes*. The book detailed the conspiracy to make both industrial hemp and marijuana illegal. For example, Herer persuasively argued that the 1937 legislation making cannabis illegal was influenced by corporate Americas, specifically the Hearst and DuPont Corporations, who viewed hemp as a threat to their timber and plastics businesses.

Steve also came to understand cannabis prohibition "has been a very powerful tool of racial repression. It was the primary purpose of the cannabis laws in the first place. If you go back and read the comments of the legislators who passed those laws, you will see there was a very clear—and by today's standards completely unacceptable—racism motivating that. And that simply got transferred as cannabis use became popular in the African-American community and moved across the country through the jazz scene." Steve argues that when looked at in a historical context and "the number of African-Americans who have been arrested and had their property taken away, you see that cannabis prohibition has been a very powerful tool of racial repression."

It's a racial reality he has witnessed firsthand with a friend from his youth, who Steve eulogized in an interview with *Mother Jones*. Steve and Eddie were typical teenage stoners. But they faced very different consequences, Steve says, because he was white and Eddie was black.

"He lived over on the other side of town from me and ended up getting busted even more than I did. And he got different treatment. When the cops found me smoking weed in the park, they took my pipe away, dumped the weed out, and told me not to let them ever see me doing it again. When the school caught me involved in cannabis transactions, they didn't invite me to come back the next year.

"When Eddie was found with weed, he was arrested and tried

and sentenced and went to juvenile hall and was suspended from school. I didn't see Eddie for a few years, and then when I finally ran into him again, he was working as a bar back at Shepherd Park, which was the local strip club. He told me it was the only place he could find a job. The club later burned down, and a friend told me how Eddie had run in twice and pulled people out of the bar before he died in the fire."

These experiences informed his activism and drove his passion for rehabilitating cannabis in the eyes of the public and lawmakers alike, through efforts like organizing the first hemp museum and touring hundreds of universities across the country to spread the cannabis gospel.

Steve says he and other activists "would do hemp teach-ins, [telling students] how this amazing forgotten product had been outlawed. We wanted to show people old stuff made from hemp but had a hard time locating things. Then I found this company in Philadelphia that had three tons of 100 percent hemp twine, which had been ordered by the Navy from Hungary in 1955. It was delivered just as the Hungarian revolution broke out, and for political reasons the Navy never accepted delivery, so the twine had been sitting in the warehouse of this company ever since."

Steve obtained balls of the hemp twine and put it into their hemp museum. Students attending their tour started offering to buy the twine. Steve admits it first sounded like more trouble than it was worth to secure more twine, but the demand became too great to ignore.

"We started getting larger orders of the twine from the company and actually selling them as a fundraising tool. And the orders got bigger and bigger. We finally realized it was the perfect macramé material, so that's how the macramé hemp jewelry fad started."

It didn't take Steve long to exhaust the supply of hemp twine in the United States, so he traveled to Eastern Europe in search of a reliable supplier. He says, "Amazingly, the same Hungarian company was still around, and they were very happy to see that there was demand from the United States again. Before long, we had a company called Ecolution that was importing container-loads of that twine."

His trip to Eastern Europe in 1990 didn't only expand his business horizons. "When I was in high school, I was ready for the Weather Underground to come hand me an AK-47. We were ready for the revolution. But it wasn't until I went to Eastern Europe a decade later and saw the consequences of communism first-hand that I lost all my vestiges of respect for a Marxist kind of economy."

Ecolution became one of the most mainstream hemp companies in the country, manufacturing hemp clothing and accessories

95

that were sold in retail stores in all 50 states and more than 20 foreign countries and proved activism and entrepreneurship can complement one another. Steve says the move into business was part of a greater plan.

"The reason I made the transition is that as an activist, I always found myself asking for funds to support the causes that were important to this movement, and I got tired of asking people for money. So, to fund our political activities, becoming an entrepreneur became a necessity. Plus, being an entrepreneur helps you create opportunities for others, through jobs, partnerships, and other projects. At the end of the day, I see activism and social entrepreneurship fighting for one goal."

Having a financial foundation also enabled Steve to pursue more ambitious activism. In 1998 Steve played a key leadership role in helping pass Initiative 59, that made medical cannabis legal in Washington DC. However, despite passing with 69 percent of the vote, US Congress—which has veto rights over Washington DC laws—blocked the initiative. Angry and disillusioned that Congress would blow off the public's will, Steve moved to California in 2000 and hit the ground running.

He became a founding member of Americans for Safe Access advocacy group for medical cannabis patients. He wrote and produced a short documentary called *For Medical Use Only*, film;

helped establish several legal cannabis gardens, and developed a new form of cannabis concentrate. But the culmination of his cannabis activism happened after Oakland granted Steve a dispensary license, enabling him to create the innovative Harborview Health Center (HHC), an innovative, medical cannabis dispensary designed to take cannabis mainstream.

"We want to make cannabis safe, seemly, and responsible," Steve said after Harborside opened. If we can't demonstrate professionalism and legitimacy, we're never going to gain the trust of our citizens. And without that trust, we're never going to get where we need to go."

Harborside opened in 2007 and was much more than a place to buy a baggie of cannabis or an edible. Among the services provided include a free holistic care clinic, chiropractic care and yoga classes, laboratory-tested products, and a low-income care package program. That same year Steve helped develop Steep Hill Labs, a cannabis analysis laboratory that performs safety screening and quality control. He says Harborside was the first dispensary to laboratory test its medicine to ensure that patients knew exactly what the cannabinoid profile was and that the cannabis was safe and not contaminated.

But Harborside's success goes beyond the services it offers. "I think first and foremost, we always focused from the beginning on our patients and creating the best patient experience in the industry," Steve says. "Our look and feel were designed to appeal to the widest range of cannabis patients possible. Then we also put a lot of emphasis on selection—raw cannabis flowers, edibles, tinctures, capsules, lotions, salves, etc.—to expand the range of choices for our patients."

Harborside's notoriety led to Discovery Channel to develop a 2011 TV series called *Weed Wars*, which followed the day-to-day operations of the dispensary. Steve saw the series as an opportunity to reach millions of Americans and change their perception of cannabis.

"The number one issue we're concerned with as far as image goes is the presentation of cannabis as a tool for wellness instead of for intoxication." And Steve acknowledges he defines wellness broadly to include enhancing the joy of living in addition to treating medical conditions.

His goal is to "help make cannabis accessible to the majority. One thing we're trying to show is that almost everyone who uses cannabis in this country uses it for wellness purposes, whether it's for cancer, or insomnia, or maybe reducing stress, or increasing creativity or libido—all are issues of overall wellness. Even talking about recreational use as a separate activity is a false dichotomy when you look at American history; in the struggle for the 40-hour workweek many doctors pointed out that for overall health and wellness, it was necessary to take a certain amount of time each week for recreation."

In a poignant irony, Steve says that cannabis brought his mother comfort before she died from Alzheimer's. "She would experience extreme distress. I would be sitting working or reading, and I would hear this long horrible wail of despair. The more I would try to calm her down, the more agitated she would get. So naturally I tried cannabis."

One night he brought her a small pipe, and she calmed after a few puffs. "It was tremendously effective for her. It just instantly brought her relief and made her more communicative. After that, whenever she saw the pipe, she'd start calming down. That was one of the few things I could do to bring her peace. It became critical to her health care."

Improving the lives of individuals remains Steve's purpose, even as cannabis evolves from a bohemian, guerilla enterprise to a growing corporate industry. Like many others, Steve has wrestled with reconciling the two.

"One of the things I have been concerned about from the beginning is that I knew as we made cannabis legal that established corporate interests would eventually try to get involved," which he admits he used to see as "an unmitigated evil. But, as I have grown older, there is nothing mainstream in the United States until it goes into the mainstream of commerce. We are not going to get the changes that we want in law and social attitudes until cannabis gains accepted space in the mainstream commercial system."

While some in the community may see it as a be-careful-what-you-wish-for scenario, Steve says it was an inevitable and necessary compromise. "It's what we set out to do. My agenda has been to protect people who care about and use cannabis because I am one of them. I've believed from the very beginning that if more people start using more cannabis and less alcohol and less tobacco and fewer pharmaceuticals, then we are going to be in a world that is more tolerant, more peaceful, in a better equilibrium with nature, has a better reverence for creativity, and understands that fun and love are important parts of life. It was never about creating a small, isolated culture that was going to percolate on its own. We wanted to change the world. So, I'm thrilled to see cannabis being mainstreamed. And it's my belief that at the end of the day, cannabis is going to influence mainstream culture more than mainstream culture is going to influence the plant."

While Steve considers big business an important aspect of cannabis acceptance, he doesn't think it will overwhelm the industry. "What I envision is a multitiered marketplace. There are lots of consumers who are going to be attracted to paying a half or a third as much as they do now for cannabis, and won't be particularly bothered that it is produced in semi-industrial factory circumstances. And there's going to be other consumers who will be happy to pay more and get something that is cultivated organically by a master gardener in a small plot. We need to make sure the regulations create an equal playing field for all these different models."

Steve believes that California will remain a global leader in both bringing cannabis to the mainstream and in driving the industry.

"I think California will become the low-cost, high-quality supplier of cannabis to most of the rest of the country and a good chunk of the rest of the world," he says. "We have some natural advantages. First, right now we are the largest legal market for legal cannabis in the world. That gives us an opportunity to build larger companies, bigger teams, more talent and sophistication, stronger brands than any other state would be able to do. We also have the perfect microclimates for growing cannabis outdoors or in greenhouses, which means we can produce a higher quality cannabis at a lower cost than any other place in the country, hands down. And we have a greater aggregation of cannabis expertise and genetics than anyplace else on the planet."

Aware that the country is at a legal, political, and cultural cannabis tipping point, Steve wrote *The Cannabis Manifesto* to tell the story of cannabis and put its legal and political checkered past in context. He dismisses the *intoxicant* label in favor of *wellness product*, using extensive research to show the biological, mental, and spiritual effect cannabis can have on human beings. It also tells readers how to get involved in the cannabis industry and how to become a better activist.

The book is also a love letter of sorts, in which he extolls cannabis's' ability to "awaken a sense of wonder and playfulness . . . enhance the flavor of a meal, the sound of music or a lover's touch."

Steve says he wrote the book for two main groups of people. "The first is people who are already in favor of cannabis reform. I wanted to give them a book that would give them all the latest science, the most up-to-date history, and the best arguments so they could be the most effective activists they could be. The second group was people who are on the fence or maybe taking a look at cannabis in a serious way for the first time. I wanted them to have a source of accurate, compelling information that was not diluted by stigma and bad science, and would enable them to get a realistic and balanced picture of this plant."

He notes that for most of his career, "I've been speaking to small audiences, handing out leaflets that nobody read, putting on demonstrations where there were more cops than protestors, sending out press releases that never got read for stories that weren't written or published. I persisted for a long time certain the day would come that the world was ready to hear the truth about cannabis [so] the opportunity to write and publish this book [was] irresistible.

Considering changing public attitudes, Steve says he expects cannabis to become federally legal after the 2020 presidential election. "But given how many US senators and representatives are coming out in support of it, I'm inclined to think it may be sooner. *The Cannabis Manifesto* has the power to speed the process."

Until then, through Harborside and his other venture, Steve will remain an outspoken advocate of the plant he believes can change the world.

The times really are a-changin', especially when it comes to the mainstreaming of cannabis. With almost half the states in the union having already legalizing medical marijuana, an increasing number of states are moving toward legalization for recreational use as well. The legal needs of the blooming cannabis industry are what prompted Denver-based Hoban Law Group to expand outside of Colorado as an international, full-service cannabis law firm, the first of its kind.

Managing partner Bob Hoban—considered the leading national expert on US cannabis law—says the legal needs of cannabis entrepreneurs and stakeholders are unique, necessitating experience and business not as usual.

"The need exists because of what happens at the beginning of an industry," he explains. "We saw this in Colorado, Washington, Oregon, and Arizona—states that we've been working in for a long time. A bunch of activist attorneys and criminal law attorneys who don't have experience practicing business and regulatory law but who are dedicated to the cause, end up becoming associated with activist and patient groups and soon start working for a lot of these companies. They are never very effective because they don't have the requisite commercial experience, and even though they are well-intentioned, they end up causing far more harm than good. That is why I have built our law firm with experienced commercial attorneys, who also deeply understand the cannabis industry and the local political scene associated with marijuana."

He says it's not uncommon for criminal defense attorneys to consider themselves cannabis attorneys. "I admire criminal defense attorneys and know a handful who we work with when those issues come up, but cannabis business owners need someone who understands trademarks, intellectual property, securities, business transactions, real estate, financial issues, and litigation—all of the different things that we do."

Bob's initial introduction to medical marijuana was personal, not professional. In 2005, doctors diagnosed his mother with pancreatic cancer, a particularly deadly form of the disease because often by the time of diagnosis, it's terminal. And even if it's not, it is difficult to treat because it's not easy to surgically remove. While his mom was undergoing chemotherapy, Bob would stop by and make her breakfast in the morning and was bothered when he saw her dependency on OxyContin.

"It just didn't sit well with me, so I ultimately started looking into our medicinal cannabis program here in Colorado. And this was before most people had any deep understanding of the countless true medicinal benefits of cannabis. Then, it was known to help you with nausea—a significant problem—take away pain, and give you an attitude adjustment for the day. Which are good things in and of themselves, particularly when your alternatives are opiates."

Bob knew his mother wouldn't smoke marijuana, so he searched for some alternative delivery methods. "And I sure as hell wasn't going to go buy some pot and make brownies or cookies; I knew that wouldn't end very well for her or it would knock her on her can, and that wasn't the position I wanted to put her in. Even though we'd had medical marijuana in Colorado since 2000, there were no dispensaries, so I looked online and found cannabis caregiver networks."

Online stores back in the day were a bit like the Wild West. "You'd call some of these phone numbers, and it would range from, *Hey man. I got the best stuff in town. Meet me at 7/11* to *Yes, Mr. Hoban, thank you for calling. My wife and I have been developing oils and tinctures.*

Needless to say, I gravitated more toward those types of people to try and find some cannabis-based product that wasn't going to knock her out."

During their conversation, Bob would talk to the business owners about what he did for a living and what the Colorado Constitution and the law in Colorado allowed for regarding medical cannabis.

"So that's how it began. I got to know growers and distributors, and they became some of my first marijuana clients. I had about a dozen clients beginning in early 2006 that were, in effect, commercial dispensaries, but they didn't have actual storefronts. They were basically delivery services, or you'd go to their house and pick things up from them—all perfectly legal under Colorado law."

The Obama presidency signaled a change, as he kept a campaign promise to make marijuana one of his administration's lowest law enforcement priorities as long as the state allowed it and had regulations in place.

"So we started to see that this was creating a perfect storm," Bob recalls. "Part of that perfect storm was also the fact that the economy was very bad in 2008. So you had a bunch of very successful entrepreneurs who were from many different walks of life looking for something else to do, and they saw this green rush coming. Around late 2008 some of my clients started to get aggressive about opening up stores."

He says their rationale was that Obama had been elected,

the economy was bad, Colorado's constitution provided them protection, and the Bush administration wasn't doing anything about medical marijuana in California. "So I helped these clients devise strategies to give them protection under state law, and in 2009 about five of my original dozen cannabis clients became some of Denver's very first dispensary owners. So, that's initially how I got into the industry on a professional level."

Bob says after Obama took office, "A large number of dispensaries were opening up all over Denver on the heels of my original clients, and there was no regulation at all. I probably ended up representing between 20 and 30 of these businesses in the early days. We were Colorado's first full-time marijuana business law firm."

To say he became known as the cannabis whisperer may be stretching it, but Bob's reputation quickly preceded him within the industry. "Not only was the word of mouth good about what I could do, but we could back it up. We're business lawyers. I've always been a commercial practitioner and a litigator, and a lot of the issues we faced had to do with real estate and business transactions. Cannabis was no longer a criminal issue in Colorado at that point, so people began to realize very, very quickly that you didn't need a criminal lawyer. Instead, you needed an experienced commercial lawyer who deeply understands the cannabis business."

One of Bob's original clients opened up a high-end dispensary called CannaMart in Centennial, Colorado. In November 2009 he ended up in Colorado State District Court seeking an injunction preventing Centennial from shutting down that dispensary.

"On December 30, 2009, the court ruled that the city could not close CannaMart on the basis of alleged federal illegality, and also said that the Colorado Constitution provided for rights for caregivers, meaning dispensaries and commercial operations. That was the case that blew it open. For the first time in US history, a court entered an injunction against a city to say: *You have to let marijuana dispensaries stay open.* Sure, California had dispensaries, but even today it's effectively black market—or, at least, a dark-grey market. The CannaMart case allowed for commercial activity. That was a first."

Bob says when he walked out of court that day, he was met by a gaggle of media. And he was happy to talk to them about the judge's decision, "He said local governments cannot choose what constitutional amendments they want to follow. He basically looked at the city's reliance on federal law as a joke, saying that cities can't enforce and should not be able to rely on federal law. The reasoning by Judge Christopher Cross was so fine and detailed I think anyone would have difficulty getting around it. It sent a message to local governments that they can't pick and choose what constitutional amendments they can abide by."

His comments made the national news. "I had friends calling me at 1:00 a.m. on New Year's Eve morning. From that point forward, we became exclusively marijuana-focused. And we began to represent countless early movers in the Colorado medical marijuana industry."

After the CannaMart ruling, Colorado lawmakers recognized that they needed to address this issue. The CannaMart case signaled the need for top-down state regulations, and the Colorado General Assembly got busy addressing the burgeoning industry, passing legislation that regulated commercial dispensaries, and explicitly allowed for commercial dispensaries. Back at the Hoban Law Group (known then as Hoban & Feola before rebranding in 2016 as part of the firm's national expansion), Bob's national exposure meant a swelling client list.

"Very, very quickly, I was seeing six and seven new clients a day for months from around the state—and around the country— about Colorado cannabis opportunities," Bob recalls. "To this day, we represent most of the largest players in Colorado that started back then and that have grown since then. Our practice has evolved from having just me and two others in 2009 to 30 lawyers as of 2016 in 15 states."

Bob says that before the CannaMart case, his commercial law firm was successful but largely anonymous. "We were good at what we did. We served as general counsel for a stable of medium-sized clients. And in fact, many of those general counsel clients are still with us. But after the court case our focus was all cannabis, all the time."

Hoban Law Group continued litigating on behalf of their cannabis clients both in Colorado and other states, representing some of the largest dispensaries and ancillary service providers to the marijuana industry. At last count, Bob has drafted more than 30 bills for the Colorado General Assembly on various issues, including for the cannabis industry.

"Today we represent many of the largest marijuana players in each marijuana-friendly state," Bob says. "We easily represent the largest hemp companies in the US and around the world that deal in industrial hemp. And now, what's really exciting, is that the people who fund both hemp and marijuana—the overall cannabis industry, what I call the *canna-business*—hire us to do their financial and securities work. Our law firm is truly a unique mergers and acquisitions law firm in the cannabis space. All of this together makes us the first real national canna-business law firm. We have also assisted a large number of cannabis companies to obtain licensure—through the application process—in each and every cannabis-legal state in the country."

The firm's website reflects the complexity of the current commercial marijuana regulatory framework. It tells prospective clients: "To obtain a license to run a commercial marijuana facility, you must first complete the registration paperwork under oath and submit it to the appropriate state and/or local licensing authorities."

Licenses are divided into several categories including:
- marijuana center licenses
- cultivation licenses
- marijuana-infused product manufacturing licenses
- occupational licenses for those with access to restricted areas of these businesses
- testing facilities

In addition to the application, plans and specifications for the proposed facility must also be submitted. "After the application is received, the state scores the submittal. And then local licensing authorities may schedule a hearing and issue public notice of the hearing as required by law. The issues that are raised by the state and local licensing authorities may include zoning, distance requirements, ownership issues, background issues, or the like."

For example, Colorado's marijuana laws have standards for buildings housing a dispensary. "The marijuana must be grown, stored, weighed, displayed or sold in a secure room, or part of the building where only those properly licensed by the state have access. Additionally, all entrances and exits to the secured area must be clearly and visibly labeled."

For those who try to navigate the regulatory maze on their own, the consequences can be personally and professionally devastating. According to information provided by Hoban Law Group, "Penalties for noncompliance with any state's regulatory scheme can be harsh and can put your business in jeopardy. Depending on the severity of the offense, penalties can include an administrative hearing, a fine, loss of licensure, or the closure of the facility. Additionally, despite many statements to the contrary, the federal government can renew its efforts to prosecute commercial marijuana businesses."

But guiding clients through the legal morass of state cannabis law is only part of Bob's involvement. His professional focus extends beyond courtrooms, licenses, and contracts to the classroom. Mindful that the rapidly changing cannabis landscape is still often misunderstood thanks to years of misinformation, much of it politics-based, Bob believes an important key to industry growth is educating the public—and sometimes lawmakers—about the benefits of cannabis and hemp. (He once represented several military veterans in a lawsuit seeking Colorado to give PTSD sufferers access to medical marijuana to treat anxiety.)

Bob, who has doctorate-level education in public policy, started teaching cannabis courses in the Law and Society program at the University of Denver as early as 2011, the first in the country to do so. "I still do that to this day. I teach public policy courses, I teach hemp courses, I teach marijuana policy courses, I teach government regulations courses that are very thick on the cannabis issues. We also have a number of research publications on the effect of cannabis as a policy on people and society and the effect of these policies on people in society." His recent publications in law and policy journals detail the successes of cannabis regulation around the world.

Bob regularly leads university-approved, for-credit research practicum courses each year studying marijuana and industrial hemp research at DU. In the summer of 2015, Bob took his educational show on the road after he was invited to guest lecture at the Catholic University of Uruguay in Montevideo, taking eleven of his DU students down with him for a joint, international cannabis study.

"Uruguay is the first country in the world to legalize cannabis and produce it through its government," he explains. "Teaching there opened many doors where I have consulted with international governments on their hemp and marijuana regulations."

In the fall of 2016, the University College at the University of Denver tapped Bob to develop a medical marijuana curriculum for their graduate healthcare leadership program—which is geared toward healthcare administrators and insurers—while still practicing law full time.

"To give you a sense of where this is going, marijuana's going to cap out around $50 or $55 billion nationally within the next five to ten years. At its core, it's a flower that you put into a pipe or a joint, and you smoke it, but that's increasingly less common as the industry develops new delivery systems. So, with [cannabis] you have to create new products for ingestion to deliver this medicine every day to remain relevant."

On the other hand, he predicts hemp will soon be a $100 billion industry. "So to me, education is the key because rational minds can help create an industry, which is what we're doing. When you create products from hemp, you're creating industrial products that already exist in the marketplace. Hemp is rope, it's clothing, it's paper, it's chemical components, it's plastics; it's building materials; very soon it's going to be irrelevant that those products are made from hemp. For example, BMW's door panels in Europe are all made from hemp. It's just a way to get a reliable product that happens to be green and environmentally friendly into the market. Our infrastructure needs to catch up, and we're getting there. And the hemp foods market is going to be tremendous in the US."

Pragmatically speaking, it's an industry that would be foolish not to encourage. Even as emerging industries still in their infancy, hemp and marijuana are proving to be an economic boom, from local communities to state coffers.

"Colorado is one of the top three economies in the country percentage-wise and has been for the last five years. You've got tens of thousands of jobs in Colorado directly related to the cannabis industry; that doesn't even count those that work exclusively in ancillary or support industries. Well over one hundred thousand people have moved to Colorado in the last nine months, and it's not just because of the mountains and the sunshine. The real estate market is off the chart. If you list a house anywhere in the Metro Denver area, it sells in three days max—and that's usually as a result of a bidding war. There were commercial areas in the city filled with vacant warehouses for at least fifteen years, if not two decades or more. Those warehouses are all full now. They have security, they have new infrastructure, there are new curbs and gutters, new paved parking lots."

Bob recently wrote an article for the *Kentucky Journal of Equine, Agriculture, and Natural Resources Law* detailing the impact of marijuana legalization, and there were very few adverse consequences. "And by the way," he adds, "teen use [of marijuana] is not up. So many other objective factors about marijuana legalization show that state government regulation of cannabis works, and it works very well. It's a healthy environment. There are so many great things to say about how this is going."

Another recent journal article in the *Journal of Social Science for Policy Implications* details the differing perspectives of marijuana in the US and Latin America.

The one big question mark remains the federal government's stance on marijuana and industrial hemp. In 2016, the federal government reasserted its position that marijuana should remain a Schedule I drug, along with heroin. But even if they bump it down to Schedule II in the near future, that may create a new set of problems for the industry.

"Even though I think most of us would agree that there are medicinal benefits to marijuana—just like there is to fish oil and green tea, for example—to call marijuana a 'medicine' is the wrong approach," Bob explains. "The term *medicinal* is problematic because it carries with it the connotation that is often confused with FDA approval and/or pharmacological recognition. This term has consumer, patient, and legal significance beyond cannabis. And it will be difficult for mainstream healthcare to grasp and/or recognize this accordingly."

He notes that as FDA-approved cannabis-based medicine evolves under a pharmaceutical model, "it is essential that we re-examine the terminology on the natural products/nutraceutical side of cannabis and look at the replacement of the word medicinal with something more akin to *wellness* or *herbal* cannabis. That will make it easier for mainstream healthcare, science, policymakers, consumers, and patients to distinguish between the two. And more importantly, it will set the table for pharmaceutical/FDA cannabis-based medicine—distributed through pharmacies—to exist side-by-side with, and exclusive of, nutraceutical and natural cannabis products produced and sold through existing state-regulated dispensaries.

Bob says the current dispensary, growth, and manufacturing systems are not going anywhere. "This is critical for the cannabis industry and policy makers to understand and adopt for patients and existing cannabis industry stakeholders. If rescheduling happens, that will not do anything with the existing natural products aspect of the industry we have today."

Bob doesn't believe there will be an outright legalization of marijuana by the US federal government in the near future. "You're going to see it develop on those two tracks that have to remain parallel and exclusive to one another because they're not the same thing, and they attract a different type of user. Just like someone might take fish oil to reduce their cholesterol, but then the other person might take Lipitor or some other pharmaceutical-based substance that reduces their cholesterol."

"They're two different things, and that's how cannabis policy and legality is going to evolve at the federal level. And we'll be ready to guide our clients and the industry as a whole through all of it."

Bob says he hopes "this wild ride" never ends because he's had the opportunity to work with numerous great entrepreneurs, risk takers, and government officials. "In the end, this is about helping people."

As of late 2016, close to 30 states had legalized cannabis for medical purposes. Of those Colorado, Oregon, Washington, Alaska, and Washington DC had also legalized recreational marijuana for adult use. After what cannabis proponents call the century-plus political demonization of the plant, public attitudes are changing at social warp speed. The business opportunities created by rapidly changing cannabis laws have created a new legal specialty, largely populated by young, creative attorneys willing to take on cannabis' regulatory Wild West, which is complicated by the federal government's continued classification of cannabis as a Schedule I drug, along with heroin and LSD.

Jana Weltzin's professional trajectory reflects the entrepreneurial spirit of her native Alaska. Born and raised in Fairbanks, Jana's law firm is one of the first in her state—and the nation—to specialize in representing cannabis startups and other industry stakeholders. On her website she notes, "Far too often we get stuck in the cycle of talking about what we want to do, could have done, or should've pursued. I never want my clients to feel like their dreams are just that—dreams." She wants to be known as "the lawyer and business advisor who not only helps create the vision but is also the driving force to execute the plan to make the vision a reality."

In 2014 Alaska voters approved Measure 2, which legalized the possession, use, and sale of marijuana for adult recreational use, which includes possession of up to one ounce of marijuana and growing up to six plants for personal use. Ironically, if it wasn't for Alaskans voting to legalize cannabis, Jana may not have returned to her home state. To pursue a career in law, she needed to head south to the lower 48.

"There are no law schools in Alaska," she explains, "so I left after high school to go get my education. I went to Chicago for my first year, played soccer there, left, and finished my undergraduate degree at University of Nevada, Reno, then got my juris doctorate at Arizona State University."

After earning her undergrad degree in political science and economics, Jana attended the Sandra Day O'Conner College of Law at Arizona State University in Tempe, Arizona, which is in the greater Phoenix metropolitan area. Jana says she picked ASU "because of its strong Indian Legal Program (ILP)."

ILPs essentially prepare future attorneys to effectively represent

Native Americans, which requires expertise in the differences between Indian Nations' legal systems and those of state and federal governments. It was a legal area she had a personal connection to.

"I grew up going to many tribal and bush communities with my dad, who's a tribal economic developer," Jana says, "and at a very young age, I interacted with the different jurisdictional issues of who governs the land. So I earned my specialization in federal land law at ASU. And land law in a roundabout way is actually how I eventually got into taking on cannabis clients."

Jana's first law job was helping negotiate compacts for the Arizona Gaming Commission with Native American tribes after her first year of law school. She worked under Mark Brnovich, who later became Arizona's attorney general in January 2015. "I was his first intern, and he was my first law boss, so it was fun," she says.

During the remainder of law school, Jana worked for different firms before landing in 2011 at the Rose Law Group, a full-service real estate and business law firm in Scottsdale that was one of the first firms in the United States to have a cannabis-specific group. It would be her professional home for the next three years. While there she was mentored by the firm's founder, Jordan Rose, in land use, which Jana notes "is a big deal in the cannabis world. You always must have a special use permit or some conditional use permit. Just like if you're going to open a bar, you have to ask the locality for permission to do it, it's the same thing with cannabis companies. So we spent a lot of time representing home developers, cannabis companies, box stores—those kinds of clients—in front of city councils or community councils. Here in Alaska we have borough assemblies; in Arizona they have counties. It's a little bit different but basically the same kind of structure."

The Rose Law Group seemed like an ideal fit, both professionally and personality-wise. Rose founded the firm as a startup doing business out of another lawyer's storage room. Within two decades it had grown to become the largest woman-owned law firm in the Southwest. The *Phoenix Business Journal* once quoted Jordan saying the thing she liked most about practicing law was "the ability to help people solve their problems." It's a sentiment Jana relates to and a purpose that would later inform her own career path. Jordan's fearless attitude resonated with Jana from the get-go.

Because of the federal government's classification of all cannabis as a Schedule I drug, states are on their own when it comes to developing rules and regulations for medical use and personal use. As a result, each state has a unique set of procedures and systems.

Jana says in Arizona, for example, the state was divided into more than one hundred community health analysis areas, or CHAA. The state assigns a certain number of licenses per CHAA based on population. The licenses are then distributed through a lottery system. One of the requirements to be eligible for the lottery is having a piece of property in the CHAA that you're applying for.

That's where a land use attorney comes in.

"You must have the right to possess," she explains. "Now, whether that's identified by a letter of intent, a lease, or you own it, you have to show that you have rights to it. That's part of your application. Now, as you can imagine, in Scottsdale a bunch of people went in for that CHAA because it's a very populated and wealthy area. Same thing for the center of Phoenix. But you have a lot of areas that aren't heavily populated, and in those places there might have been only one or two applications for a license. So your odds in a lottery for those licenses were a lot better." Currently, there are 124 active licenses in Arizona, which are fully integrated. "Meaning you don't need to apply for separate licenses to retail, manufacture, or cultivate. You can do all three underneath your license.

"However," Jana points out, "you cannot grow marijuana without having an open retail dispensary with a set number of hours. You can have a retail without a cultivation facility, and you can buy some marijuana and products from other licensees, but you cannot grow without having your own dispensary. Same thing with a kitchen. You cannot have a separate location where you're manufacturing oils, edibles, [and] all those kinds of goods without having a cultivation. Now, you don't need to have your store at that location, it can be offsite, but you do need to have a store to do cultivation and manufacturing."

Jana says this intersection of law and practicality is where entrepreneurial ingenuity lives. "It doesn't make sense for everybody to grow because not everybody is a gardener, and a lot of people kill green things. I know I can't keep anything alive. The same skill set for growing isn't necessary for being a baker who just wants to produce edibles. So, we saw kitchens popping up that were associated with a license, and they had a storefront at some location, but their cultivation area—which by law they had to have—was like three plants. People can be very creative to get around the legal obstacles."

Jana believes the regulatory environment, such as the FDA's recent determination that cannabis-derived oils cannot be categorized as a food supplement, is a constant challenge for cannabis entrepreneurs. "How do you expect to take this industry out of the black market when they make it so difficult to run a business, and you feel like you're continually punished?" She also suggests there's some hypocrisy at play. "The federal government says: *We don't think this has any medical value, and we don't want you states to say it has any medical value either*, yet the federal government has patents on a number of THC cannabinoids structures. But it's a process. We're just getting through the prohibition period and coming into the light."

Like most cannabis industry pioneers, Jana believes the more educated the public becomes about the sustainability of hemp plants, the more perceptions will change. While most recent state regulation has centered on the medicinal and recreational use of various cannabis varieties, the strains bred for industrial use, called hemp, are among the most sustainable plants on earth. For example, one acre of hemp produces as much fiber as two to three acres of cotton. Hemp fiber is stronger, softer, and more durable than cotton. One acre of hemp annually will produce as much paper as two to four acres of trees. All types of paper products—from tissues to cardboard—can be produced from hemp.

Hemp can also be used to produce strong, durable, and environmentally-friendly plastic substitutes. Mercedes Benz has begun manufacturing automobile bodies and dashboards made from hemp. Hemp seeds, which do not cause a drug high, contain a protein that is more nutritious and more economical to produce than soybean protein. And just as corn can be converted into clean-burning ethanol fuel, so can hemp.

Jana admits clients can sometimes get frustrated by the system and bureaucrats who still demonize cannabis. "I tell them that I've been on this earth for 29 years, and I knew at a very young age that all the rhetoric about cannabis was bullshit. My parents were enlightened. They taught me well. But imagine being 65 and having been told something is evil over and over again your entire life. Having that drilled into your head. And then imagine one day somebody says your entire belief structure is fake. I would personally have a hard time with that. There's always the perception versus reality—90 percent perception, 10 percent reality. If people knew 100 percent of the reality, this wouldn't even be a debate. And I wouldn't have a job," she laughs.

Jana's road back to Alaska began when the state legalized cannabis in November 2014. Looking back, it seems more destiny than design.

"The day I got hired," Jana relates, "one of the Rose Law Group partners, Ryan Hurley, who happened to lead the cannabis group, went into Jordan's office and told her he'd had a dream the night before that Alaska legalized, and the firm expanded to Alaska. He didn't even know I'd been hired yet, and he certainly didn't know I was from Alaska. When I heard about his dream, I thought it was cool, but at that point I didn't know if I even wanted to go back to Alaska."

Fast-forward three years. In November 2014 Alaska legalized and Jana and Ryan are talking strategy. "We knew California was coming online too, and the firm had changed its tune from wanting to focus on Alaska. Instead, they wanted the focus on California and to capture Alaska from afar. I said: *Well, look; here's the deal: I'm going to Alaska.*"

Her bosses agreed and asked her to start a Rose Law Group Alaska office. Jana says she spent the next six months immersing herself in the Alaska cannabis industry to start developing a network of connections. "I infiltrated the Coalition for Responsible Cannabis Legislation and lobbied during the 2014 sessions to get House Bill 123 through, which created the Marijuana Control Board. Then I packed up my house in Arizona, put it all in a U-Haul pod, and drove from Phoenix, through Denver, and then up to Alaska at the end of August 2015."

Not long after Jana established the Rose Law Group's Alaska office, she had a personal and professional epiphany. "Alaska is my home state, but there I was shipping all the money and the development I was creating out of state, and it seemed backward to me. So, I decided: *If I'm going to do this, if I'm going to come up here and teach people how to start their businesses, help them, guide them, I might as well have some experience starting a business myself. If I'm going to ask my clients to put their butts on the line, I should probably do it myself.* So, I quit Rose Law Group, and I started my own company: JDW, LLC."

Jana says her bosses were disappointed by the split but probably not overly surprised. "They're a classy firm, they're classy people, and they understood. In fact, Jordan left the mid-sized firm she was working at and started her firm at 29, so when I turned 29, I remember her looking at me like: *Shit, it's your 29th birthday,*" she laughs. "Jordan is definitely somebody I look up to; she's definitely inspired me to be able to do this, and I learned so much at Rose Law Group. I couldn't have done it without that background. That being said, she's a business woman, and in her eyes that was a loss. But I do feel it was an amicable split. And that's how it should be. You either create the opportunity for the best and brightest to become the best, brightest version of themselves within your company, or you teach them what you can and hope they'll be friendly competition."

Jana's decision to go from an associate at an established firm to startup entrepreneur was like embarking on a professional high-wire act with no net. "I totally winged it," she laughs. "I'm still winging it. I started with just my laptop out of my home office." But what she lacked in infrastructure she made up for with old-fashioned drive. "I did a lot of speaking events. I became involved in the community, got involved in assembly meetings, testified at the legislature, wrote articles, and did a lot of radio interviews."

Her articles staked out her position as a defender of the small business owner and often challenged lawmakers to eliminate some of their regulatory hurdles. In an article she wrote for *Marijuana Venture*, Jana noted: "Due to the lack of traditional banking services, cannabis business owners face a cash management and security disaster. Cannabis appears to be the only state-sanctioned business whose financing ability is restricted to individual private loans that are usually unsecured and subject to extremely high interest rates.

What other market faces this type of service discrimination?

"The consequences of such discrimination are a lose-lose for all. The state loses out on potential tax revenue as cash is more difficult to track; cannabis businesses are unable to utilize banking services to track money in and out; large stockpiles of cash at the businesses puts employees at risk of being a target for criminals; banks lose out on a substantial amount of business. Also, because the opportunities for traditional lending services are nonexistent or very limited, private individuals who do loan funds to cannabis-related companies could easily have connections to crime groups. The federal government is undermining its priorities by restricting the ability of cannabis companies to do business with regulated financial institutions."

While Jana's firm represents non-cannabis clients as well, her vigorous defense of small businesses and numerous media appearances put her on the cannabis industry radar. "When people said: *Hey, Jana, will you come sit on a marketing panel?* I just said yes. And I continue to say yes. As soon as you stop saying yes, they'll stop calling. Yes, it eats up a lot of time but you get a lot back. There was a lot of word of mouth. Cannabis law is new. I was the only show in town that had any experience in these things. It's like what they say about being in a small pond. That definitely helped."

She's very aware, though, that things will change sooner rather than later. "A lot of lawyers are going to realize pretty soon that this is just regular business law, regular real estate planning law with a little twist on it. Hopefully, they won't figure it out for a while, but they are going to figure it out. The competition will grow."

But Jana has a good head start. After just eight months in business, her firm already handles nearly all the top local players in Alaska and also has clients in Arizona, Washington, and Oregon.

"I got the majority of my clients by just word of mouth, and it snowballed to the point where I have a waiting list now because I want just to focus on what we have."

Her growing business means she can no longer be a one-woman show working from home. "Now we're legit. We have a real office, and I hired a full-time paralegal to handle the administrative work, which was eating up 40 to 50 percent of my time. And I'm not good at it. So it was a real lose-lose proposition." She also has a part-time associate who helps with contracts. "When I feel the time is right, I'll probably bring her on full time. It's all about sustainability. Talking the talk is one thing, being able to produce and get people results is another."

To that end, Jana notes that as of September 2016, she has a perfect record so far in helping her clients get their licenses approved, securing more than 20 licenses. Jana has secured everything from permits for testing labs to unlimited cultivation licenses. Her expertise also resulted in the mega-canna legal enterprise, Hoban Law Group (see Chapter TK), approaching her to be of counsel to them on cannabis-related issues, which she accepted. But Jana is quick to point out that her end goal isn't to be the biggest.

"I would like just to make it sustainable, a little bit more autonomous. I'd like to be able to bring some people in that can help keep things flowing, so I don't necessarily have to work 80 hours a week or touch every document that goes out."

While she might not want to be the biggest, she does want to be the most effective, especially for the local cannabis community. "It's an interesting thing about de-scheduling marijuana completely on a federal level. On one side of the coin, it's great because people won't go to jail. But from a business point of view, what other industries do you know of where you can get in on the ground floor as a mom-and-pop business—most of my clients are families—and actually make a stab at it? Get a chance to create something that is larger than what you thought you could create before? There's no other industry where that's been possible in our lifetime.

"And the reason we can do it is there's that risk. There's a risk of federal prosecution. The reason small businesses like mine and those of my clients can thrive and succeed is that we are willing to take the risk, willing to put ourselves out there and face federal prosecution. The big boys—Marlboro, Parliament, you name it—don't want to get into the industry because they have too much to lose if the feds change their tune, which is always possible. But we're willing to take the risk. That's our advantage. So, if you de-schedule marijuana and legalize it federally, that risk goes away, and our advantage disappears. So I want to focus on getting strong state-wise. Getting our local businesses up and sustainable to the point where should cannabis become legalized federally, then at least the mom-and-pop businesses need to be bought out; the big boys won't be able just to push them out."

Jana says that focus on promoting local small business has always been an integral part of the cannabis movement.

"It's huge. And it's the reason why I'm in it: to create local sustainability. We lived through a couple of recent recessions, and even people my age understand that the national economy can affect people on the most local level. So, if I can help people find some way to create a little bit of sustainability within our local economies, that's a good thing."

MEDICALLY CORRECT

Medically Correct started in 2010, and the incredibles brand has grown into Colorado's highest-volume edibles company by investing in developing a proprietary extraction and manufacturing system that focuses on delivering the highest quality cannabis and organic ingredients in the most consistently delicious edible on the market. After nearly six years of investing in state-of-the-art manufacturing and quality control processes, incredibles is going national.

It might not take a village to build a successful cannabis business, but in the case of Medically Correct, the parent company of incredibles, it took the serendipitous coming together of three unlikely partners to create one of the country's leading edibles companies.

The story starts in Council Bluffs, Iowa, where Rick Scarpello grew up. "My dad was a barber, and we lived paycheck to paycheck. We weren't poor but not very well-to-do either, that's for sure.

Fortunately, my dad was able to take us on vacation every year. We'd jump into the family station wagon and drive to Denver to visit my mother's relatives. I fell in love with the city of Denver and with Colorado and knew one day I was going to come live here."

Rick says he always had an entrepreneurial spirit, even when holding down salaried jobs. He also had a knack for management. "I started my management career in Council Bluffs, Iowa, at a restaurant called Romeo's where I was the general manager at 19 years old with 30 employees."

After two years Rick left to work at La Fonda de Acebo, a restaurant in Omaha, Nebraska, that was based out of Denver. "I was hired as a general manager, and they sent me to Denver for training. While there I met the owner and asked: *I would just like to stay here. Do you have a manager's job available here?* He put me to work, and so I stayed in Colorado and never left."

From there Rick held management positions at various companies, including Brunswick. "I was an avid bowler as I grew up. For about six years I managed Brunswick Bowling, where I won Manager of the Year awards. I put up black lights, music, and fog machines and started this thing called Rock-n-Bowl, leading them to change their name to Brunswick Zone and changing the way people enjoy bowling. I eventually became a partner at Chesapeake Bagel Bakery. We continued to grow, moving from one location to five in just six years. We made bagels in one location and shipped them to the other locations."

At the bagel company Rick learned about baking and recipes and transporting refrigerated dough, leading to his next job at Il Fornaio bakery where he stayed for seven years. "I was the regional director of operations of a large plant with one hundred employees that serviced clients locally in Denver. To get more customers, I started a frozen bread program to build sales nationally and build my paycheck. Il Fornaio never did frozen bread in 30 years of business, and I was pushing them in a new direction. I had to learn about food safety plans, food defense plans, and third-party audits on food safety. There I mastered large-scale, FDA-compliant food production processes. Food safety and food defense plans became my specialty. Il Fornaio only does frozen bread now."

While at Il Fornaio, Rick met a packaging vendor named Bob Eschino who became his guy. Rick could never have imagined that Bob would also eventually become his introduction to the wonderful world of cannabis as medicine.

After six years at Il Fornaio, Rick's next stop was Udi's Bakery, where he was the originator of Udi's gluten free. At Udi's, Rick and Bob continued their professional relationship, but it wasn't until an encounter with Bob's grandmother that Rick was inspired to undertake a new career path.

"When Rick was at Udi's, we were always throwing around ideas of what we could do as a side business," Bob recalls. "And typically it revolved around food because he had access to this giant kitchen that we could manufacture out of and I was the packaging guy. My brother had become the caretaker for my grandmother and started giving her medical marijuana, which helped with her appetite. Her hands were all arthritic and in pain, and he brought her topical THC lotions and fed her edibles. And a light bulb went off."

Bob researched edibles and discovered "it wasn't treated like food, and it wasn't treated like medicine. People made these things out of their house, wrapped them in Saran wrap, and put a little handmade label on them. There were no nutritional or food facts. And on the medicinal part, nobody tested the oil. Six years ago they had no idea what the potency of these edibles was. I found that people were afraid of edibles because you could have an edible one week from a manufacturer, and you would be fine then you would have the same edible from the same manufacturer the following week, and you were over medicated. Nobody had any idea what they were putting in there. That was our opportunity: to focus on consistency, quality ingredients, and incredibly clean extracts."

Bob realized that Rick's expertise was perfecting a recipe and duplicating it thousands of times. "So, I went to Rick and said: *Hey, let's start a cannabis company.* He thought I was crazy at first."

Then Rick met Bob's grandmother.

"She was dying, and Bob showed me how cannabis was positively affecting her at the end of her life," Rick says. "She'd eat a quarter of a cookie, and it would help her have a little bit of pain relief. Or she'd eat a half a cookie, and she'd get an appetite. And then she'd eat a whole cookie and sleep for four or five hours straight, which she'd never do on any other pharmaceutical. It was amazing what cannabis did for her, at the end of her life. Up until then I didn't know that it was medicine."

After meeting Bob's grandma Rick was a believer. "I said: *We've got to do this. I know how to make 20,000 muffins a day, so why can't we make that many medicated treats? I know how to automate, you know packaging, you know buying food ingredients, you know wholesale distribution, I know wholesale distribution—let's be wholesalers.*"

Rick and Bob opened up a little kitchen—and struggled for the next year and a half. Until a chance meeting with Derek Cumings changed the direction of their business. They realized the secret ingredient wasn't just quality ingredients and processes but also creating the industry's best extractions.

Derek Cumings, a fifth-generation Coloradoan, admits as a young man he "bought into the prohibition of marijuana." But he began rethinking his position when Amendment 20, Colorado's first legalization effort—for medical marijuana—was put on the ballot in 2000.

"I remember wondering: *Man, how can they deny people with AIDS, or people with cancer at the end of their life, this treatment? What harm is it going to do? Of course they deserve to be able to try this as an option.* So, I made flyers and handed them out in support of Amendment 20. It would take me years to realize that it wasn't just for dying people; quality cannabis can heal in many ways. I only hope to help shed light on this truth through legal means."

That epiphany was personal. When Derek was younger, he had fallen off a cliff and broken both legs. Although he didn't know it at the time, the impact also injured his lower spine, which manifested five years later. Once diagnosed, doctors recommended that Derek have his L4 and L5 vertebrae fused to his tail bone.

"So, I lost 50 percent or more of the height on three discs in my lower spine, and they started treating me with painkillers. Here I was, a young man in my mid-20s taking 25 different pills with 13 different prescriptions. The side effects of which continued to increase and compound. One day while driving I started having back spasms, so I took what I thought were my muscle relaxers. I ended up running off the road because I had taken sleeping pills by mistake."

Derek's situation became desperate, and he didn't know how he could do this the rest of his life.

Then a friend gave Derek some tincture, and it changed his life forever. "The next day I called the doctor and told him I didn't want my anti-nausea pill anymore, which I had to take because of all the other medication I was on. The tincture worked so instantaneously on the nausea that I was able to eat again and wasn't worried about being sick in public from my pain medication. Since I wasn't worried about getting sick in public, I stopped having anxiety, so I didn't need the anti-anxiety pill. Next, I didn't need the anti-depressant anymore because the only reason I was depressed was because I wasn't leaving my house over the anxiety of throwing up in public."

Using the tincture enabled Derek to systematically eliminate one prescription after another. "I got down to only needing a muscle relaxer for pain management from the consistent muscle spasms I have in my back. I changed from taking hundreds of painkillers a month down to 30 painkillers a month. I went from 25 pills a day to three or two pills a day, and that was proof enough for me to change my lifestyle and my path with cannabis."

Because he'd been injured on the job, his workman's comp insurance called the shots. They were made aware every time he added a new cannabis treatment, resulting in a reduction of the number of prescriptions he was given. So, one day Derek's physician informed him he'd have to undergo a urine test, and that they would drop him as a patient if he tested positive for cannabis. "And I was: *Wait a minute…of course I'm going to fail.* He told me they would not be able to provide me with prescriptions anymore because of my 'drug-seeking behavior.' I asked: *What drug-seeking behavior? I ripped up my morphine script in front of you. You guys were killing me with drugs. Now I saved myself with weed, and you're telling me I can't use weed?* This was a truly heartbreaking moment in my life."

This experience became the catalyst that motivated Derek's new life's work. He had to take his health into his own hands.

"I found a partner, and we opened up one of the first 10 dispensaries in Colorado, and it was all based on the edibles that I was taking, like the tincture. People were still ignorant back in the day. They called it liquid weed because nobody knew what it was. I now believe more people are accepting that cannabinoids are a vitamin, are healthy. We're only just now learning that human beings should have a cannabinoid-rich diet, I can't wait for research to support what advocates already know."

As he learned to make his own tincture, he realized the importance of quality control and product consistency so people could count on what they were using. Derek says at the time many of the dispensaries were just fronts for dealing baggies of weed or crumbled brownies in a sack.

Derek thought: *Man, if somebody just put this stuff in a package and put the ingredients on it and tried to make quality products, they could really do something good here.*

Derek concentrated on developing high-quality edibles, and developing a proprietary process was the priority. Growth, however, was limited because he made his products—mostly cannabis candy bars—in his condo, and Colorado regulations made starting a legitimate commercial medical marijuana kitchen very difficult.

Derek teamed up with a woman who wanted to open a dispensary but didn't know enough about cannabis or edibles or concentrates to do it on her own. She offered him a 50-50 partnership; Derek was in charge of operations, and his partner did the business development. Derek's dream came true; he was fulfilling his passion by opening a dispensary in his hometown.

Initially, they were a big fish in a very small cannabis pond, but soon competition became much fiercer. "The first couple of months we're all fine and dandy, and then all of a sudden hundreds of my customers were trying to open up their own stores. As that boom happened, regulations cinched down on dosing and packaging. Our store had been open and paying taxes for two years when they amended state law so individual municipalities could ban and opt out of medical marijuana, and so that's what happened. They closed my garden; they closed my shop. I wasn't doing anything illegal, but they just said: *You're closed.* I couldn't believe it was all over, and that they'd cheated me out of my cannabis opportunity."

In the red $150,000 from loans taken out to start the dispensary, Derek did consulting work and eventually dug himself out of his financial hole. And then by chance, he met Rick and Bob and offered them some business advice.

"I told them: *Look, quality ingredients—and therefore products— are all that matters. If you consistently deliver on potency and test from the beginning, you'll deliver a following. Prices are going to continue to go up for people that are trying just to buy weed and make it into a product. Weed prices are going to go down for people that grow their own weed and do their own manufacturing. So, I recommend you guys get a garden as soon as you can.* Literally, there was an edible company opening every single week. They needed to be able to compete. Also, even though they were making the best weed brownie I've ever had, they were going to run into hurdles like shelf life and longevity that were going to be too high to jump when there are other people able to accommodate that."

As Derek got to know Bob and Rick's process, the more impressed he became. "Rick understood sourcing of ingredients. He understood homogeneity of large batch recipes. He understood scaling recipes from something small to an industrial level, while Bob understood packaging and labeling. I start thinking that those guys were the ones that could make candy bars the right way. A match made in heaven."

In the year he had been out of business, Derek fielded many offers from former competitors trying to get his recipes, but he could never make a deal because none of the operators met his quality standards. "Half were operating in a garage. I believed my products could be the biggest thing in the world; I dreamt of seeing my products in a locked cabinet at 7-11; I wanted my products at every liquor store. So, I wasn't going to give it up to just anybody. Then when I met Rick, I realized he had the capacity to do what I had dreamed about. I was: *Man, this is the guy.*"

The next time Derek spoke with Rick and Bob, he encouraged them to forget about the brownies and carrot cake and start manufacturing Derek's confections. When asked what he wanted in compensation, Derek said he wanted to be part of the company— at some point. In other words, he let them have the recipes for free in exchange for a promise.

"People told me I was crazy. *I can't believe you just gave your shit away*. But I didn't give it away. I shook two people's hands and said let's figure it out later. I wasn't going to charge them a bunch of money for something they couldn't afford. I'd seen their potential and trusted that these were good men. I thought if nothing else, my product was going to make it out there. Delivering delicious, potent products was the only mission."

For the next several years Derek worked with and for various companies, watching Rick and Bob grow their business from afar. Finally, the day came in 2014 when Rick offered to put Derek in charge of the garden and the lab and make him an official part owner of the company, which has succeeded beyond his imagination.

"The Mile-High bar has been available in Colorado since 2008. I never dreamed incredibles would become so big. It used to be my little sister and me manufacturing eight or 12 bars at a time. Now we have batches of four thousand bars, done in hours. It was just my sister helping me part-time through college, now I've got 60-some employees, and I'm hiring five new people this week. I'm not in every 7-11, but I know we're sold to seven hundred licenses, more than five hundred Colorado dispensaries. Our market saturation with the candy bars has made it to 95 percent; they're truly available everywhere. And it came about to make people understand that cannabis is a good alternative to so many problematic medications that we use in our lives. Before I go to my eight o'clock morning meeting, instead of taking pills I take cannabis, and I'm able to walk still."

And with the company's growth and success, Derek sees them coming full circle. "I think at some point I'd like to try and put out that carrot cake and that brownie because they were so good."

Rick says their process keeps refining. "I know we make some of the best cannabis extracts in the world and are getting increasingly sophisticated, and we're now actually separating CBD from THC. We've opened an extraction company, and out of that we've now opened a manufacturing company called the Incredible Extractor that makes machines. We designed the hardware for cannabis extraction because nobody else was. The machines for food are too big; they won't even fit in my office."

Bob says in addition to selling cannabis, education about hemp and safe cannabis consumption is one of their company's missions. "I've learned so many amazing things about this plant over the last six years, and I am convinced more and more that it is one of the most therapeutic plants on the planet. Part of the reason I joined this business is to lobby through private business, to lead through example with my work, pay taxes, and contribute to helping change the paradigm of cannabis use across the country. I want to set an example through my companies' best practices to encourage regulators and my peers to take us seriously, enforce quality standards, and progress research. If you're getting cannabinoids in your system, your body's working better. So, we can help everything from a headache to a toe ache and everything in between because your body becomes more efficient when getting cannabinoids. Every cell in your body has a CB1 and a CB2 receptor, and those receptors are only looking for cannabinoids. If we didn't need cannabinoids in our system, why does every cell in our body look for it?"

Bob notes that up until the government made marijuana—and by extension hemp—illegal, "We used hemp and hemp oil for just about everything, including feedstocks, so our animals and our food supply were enriched with CBDs and cannabinoids. But when we made hemp oil and cannabinoids illegal in the '30s and took that out of our diet, look at how illnesses have shot up since that point. I guarantee there is a direct correlation in that."

Like Derek and Bob, Rick believes in the health benefits of cannabis and its importance to humanity's overall wellness. You could almost say he's evangelical about it (pun intended). "Tylenol kills 150 people a year. Tobacco results in 600,000 deaths a year in America. Forty-one people will die today from alcoholism, and it is a non-scheduled drug. Yet cannabis is a Schedule I drug. The number one addiction is to opiates, which kill people but are prescribed every day."

After nearly eight years, developing proprietary processes and products has paid off. Incredibles has managed to become the highest-volume and most loved cannabis company in Colorado without investing in marketing, but by instead investing in potency, taste, and safety.

The company mission statement is simple: "Incredibles is

excited to spend the next few years pivoting towards national thought-leadership in the cannabis industry, refining our brand, and elevating our national PR presence and product line. Incredibles will be in Oregon, Nevada, California and Puerto Rico. Consistency and quality are the promise of incredibles. We've developed proprietary processes with owned genetics and will bring our truly delicious and trusted products across the country in the coming days. We want to be at the forefront of helping to spread alternative approaches to wellness and health and happiness and encourage the medical community, regulators, and consumers to help end the unjust war on cannabis and boost our economy at the same time."

NEW FRONTIER

By any measure, cannabis in the United States is poised to be the next great growth industry. The FDA be damned, red and blue states alike are laying the groundwork for both medical and recreational business opportunities as voters across the nation support legalizing the long-maligned plant. It's a boon not only to the overall economy but to female entrepreneurs, who are finding the cannabis world an easier place to make professional inroads than many other industries.

Giadha DeCarcer, founder and chief executive officer of data analysis firm New Frontier—often referred to as the *Bloomberg* of the cannabis industry—reports that 25 percent of cannabis business owners are women. And according to *Marijuana Business Daily*, women account for 36 percent of executives in the cannabis market.

"The cannabis industry is so new that there are very few barriers to get in, especially for women," Giadha says. In a CNN Money profile, she called the cannabis industry "a clean slate where people with drive and education have a chance to succeed on their own merit. It is also inherently more open-minded than some, and women may have a special affinity for the nurturing and healing aspect of cannabis."

Perhaps more to the point, Giadha notes that the cannabis industry doesn't have the same persistent glass ceiling still present in other sectors such as banking and technology. "Those are all heavily male dominated areas, so it makes it harder to rise to the top," she says. "That was the biggest frustration for me. Having gender parity is important in any industry, it is not specific to the cannabis sector. Gender—as well as cultural and background diversity—in any team leads to better decisions."

She speaks from first-hand knowledge. Before launching New Frontier in 2014, Giadha grew up, professionally speaking, in traditional corporate America. Her journey was made that much more difficult being an immigrant. Born in Italy and raised in France and Spain by to her diplomat father and Cuban-born actress mother, Giadha didn't come to the United States until she was 17, during her last year in high school.

Although fluent in four languages at the time, she didn't speak any English but quickly tapped into the American dream and ethos that you can achieve anything if you're willing to work hard enough for it. It took seven years of effort, beginning with an A.A. from Miami Dade Community College and a bachelor's degree from the University of Pennsylvania. She later earned her master's at Georgetown. University.

Giadha started her career in late 1999 as an associate at JP Morgan doing mostly data analysis and collection for the financial sector in New York and London. And then the terrorist attack of September 11 happened. "Unfortunately, most of the people in my office died that day. I was very lucky because I was late to work."

Not long after she shifted away from investment banking and moved to Washington, DC, to pursue her master's degree and to join the War on Terror. "I ended up working for the government, again doing data collection," she says. "I had the opportunity after doing that to work in technology and energy at Washington Policy & Analysis, applying rigorous data collection and analysis to help Fortune 100 companies figure out opportunities and risks in various sectors."

A self-described serial entrepreneur, Giadha left government work and founded her first data company, GNI International, in 2007. The company's wireless solution monitored driving behavior for safety and efficiency. "We had the first patent pending on Snapshot, a little gizmo that was connected in your car and monitored real-time driving behavior to assess the risk of that particular driver and therefore calibrate premiums. But that didn't work out so much for us because it was in 2008 just as the economy crashed."

After GNI couldn't afford to renew its patent, Progressive Car Insurance came out with a comparable version two weeks after GNI's patent pending expired. "Progressive was able to work it out," Giadha says with a verbal shrug. "We ... not so much. But the experience was my first real entrepreneurial effort combining the data collection, data analytics, and technology components."

Fast forward six years. Giadha was running a consulting firm she founded that helped US companies going to emerging markets by providing risk assessments, opportunities, and notifications through data collection and data analysis. In 2014 a friend called Giadha asking her to assess the opportunity and the risk regarding a cannabis venture. He was interested in taking advantage of Maryland issuing medical marijuana licenses and wanted her help in devising a business plan.

"I did what any investor would do, any business person would do," Giadha says. "I looked at the data, and I found there no industry report nor was there any data," even though it was a multi-billion-dollar industry. "There was no research with methodological standards that would allow you to take the data in it seriously. There was no one collecting data for this interesting and apparently really promising industry—at least, not with the type of rigor that we're used to in government, technology, and banking. And no one was able to report in a quantifiable, valid manner even just the size of the market."

Also, she notes, "The industry is not very sophisticated right now in even understanding it needs data. Owner-operators who have the data are mom-and-pop shops that don't get the value of actionable intelligence to support their business. And so a new company was born in 2014 to fill a gap."

Not everyone was quick with an *atta girl*. "I have to tell you, most people thought we were crazy, that I was crazy," Giadha laughs. "There was a lot of stigma. But the way we looked at it was, here's a plant that has medicinal, recreational, and industrial application. It's going to be a worldwide phenomenon, and someone has to have access to good data, which is the lifeblood that fuels any industry. So I made the transition to the cannabis industry."

Giadha has described New Frontier as being comprised of "statisticians, econometricians, and data geeks." The company provides analyst reports through partners and via its website, offers a subscription to a data visualization tool called Equio. According to the website Equio "gives you real-time insight into your sales data along with comparisons with actual sales throughout your regions" and does custom research for clients including investors, legislators, and operators.

As Giadha notes, with dozens of states (and counting) and the District of Columbia legalizing consumption in one form or another, "It's important that data support business models and shape legislation. Today cannabis is a $5 billion industry, growing at the rate of 27 percent per year, the fastest growing industry in the country."

While multinational financial institutions may consider big data integral to success in the global marketplace, small startups in an industry that is slowly going legit after decades of legal demonization may have a harder time understanding the value or need of data. But Giadha says it is just as—or even more helpful— for entrepreneurs at all levels.

"We are at our core a big data solutions provider. Big data entails velocity, diversity, and volume of data. What that means is that we collect, ingest, and report in real time millions and millions of data points and then provide the information to our customers— operators as well as in investors and researchers—in a way that is digestible. We collect anything: energy costs and transaction data, what consumers want, what brand is trending, what state has more revenue, market size—all those data points are collected by us in real time. We can then package that data in various ways."

One way is a report. Giadha says New Frontier sets the standard for understanding what the industry is like from a quantifiable perspective: the size, the protocols, the space, drivers, dynamics, etc.

"We also provide custom research to investors and operators that need a deeper dive for a particular challenge or to raise capital," Giadha says. "Finally we offer a platform, Equio, which is the purest form of our big data solution offering. This platform enables us to provide all those millions of data points that we collect to the operators in an interactive manner, in an easily digestible manner, in a manner that applies to their actual business."

She gives an example: suppose a dispensary owner has more than one location in a particular region. "The Equio platform instantaneously shows them how each of their locations is doing in some of the gross sales, so they can immediately assess the performance of each of those businesses. And then it gives them the ability to compare their growth sales average so they can also instantaneously see how they're performing against competitors. If they see that one of their locations is underperforming—when compared to their other locations or compared to the regional average—we can then show them how each of the products offered in that dispensary is performing across the board. We compare it to other products in that store and other products in other stores. And we compare it to how that product is selling for competitors in the region. Lastly, we give the dispensary owner the ability to replace a low performing product one that is buzzing and in demand in real time in their region."

New Frontier tracks buzz through about 2.5 million data points from Twitter, Instagram, and other social media platforms. The Equio platform bases the comparison with competitors' businesses on regional averages of gross sales. "The way we do that," Giadha explains, "is through customers that subscribe to our portal, which integrates with their point of sale solution, so we get all the transaction data, and then we aggregate it."

Beyond providing data to help individual companies large and small grow, Giadha also hopes to help shape social, political, and cultural perceptions. She says the company's mission is to bring transparency and legitimacy to the cannabis industry by empowering decision makers with data-based facts.

In an interview with MaryJanes.com, she said, "I would hope and expect policy and lawmakers to ask questions and make educated decisions based on all the facts." She also advocates green practices in the industry. "Cannabis is the most energy intensive agricultural commodity in our economy due to the significant energy costs associated with indoor cannabis cultivation. The transition to greenhouse and outdoor production can lower energy use by as much as 90 percent by replacing artificial light with sunlight and by reducing the need for climate control systems. Developing regulations that allow for the most flexible and energy efficient cultivation techniques, including outdoor cultivation, will be critical to the long-term sustainability of cannabis production."

Perhaps most important is her desire to help break the glass ceiling. "Providing authoritative data, analytics, and targeted solutions enables decision makers and operators in the cannabis industry to be aware of the quantifiable risks associated with the lack of parity, social justice, and environmental awareness, not only for their businesses but the industry and nation as a whole. While we can't force decisions, we can certainly do our part in providing those decision makers with the truth."

Giadha's desire to see changes in the laws criminalizing marijuana stems is personal. She recalls the day she got a phone call from her brother's girlfriend telling her he was in prison for growing cannabis at his home.

"I had no idea," she says. "My brother was my emergency contact. He never told me anything because obviously, he knew better than to tell me. But the tragedy of all that is my brother had an absolutely clean record. But because he was growing pot in Florida the court gave him the maximum sentence of three-and-a-half years in a maximum security correctional facility. Listen; yes, he did something wrong and broke the law. I believe in our government and the justice system, so he had to pay for what he did, But the tragedy is that the level of the punishment drastically exceeded the seriousness of the crime because of geography. And he is spending his sentence with serial killers and other [hardened and dangerous criminals]."

So while she admittedly launched the company because she saw a golden potential business opportunity, close behind was the chance to provide valid information to legislators, law enforcement, and others.

"My team and I are truly committed to share information and educate all stakeholders associated with this industry whether it is regulators or lawmakers or financial institutions or operators. There is a lot of ignorance that has negatively impacted and permanently damaged lives such as that of my brother and my family and others who need the medicine cannabis can offer but have been unable to get it. That's my personal angle."

Starting new companies may have provided Giadha professional purpose and fulfillment, but she admits her romantic life was lagging behind. So at the same time she was launching New Frontier, she challenged herself to find personal happiness as well. "I was about to turn 40, I was single with no children, and I was sort of dissatisfied," she says, recounting how her ex-boyfriend ended their relationship for working too much on her business.

Giadha raised money on Kickstarter for a docu-series, *Love & Business—90 Days to Launch*, that followed her efforts to find success in business and love—the ultimate life balance. In the trailer she says, "This is not a drama, reality TV, Kardashian-meets-Jersey-Shore. It's nutty, it's fun, it's engaging, it's smart—and most importantly, it's real. Some shit you can't make up. True story."

The series followed her quest to find a relationship within 90 days while simultaneously launching New Frontier. The underlying goal was to explore the challenges women face in balancing career and family. It was a subject close to her heart. After establishing GNI International, she also founded WeR, which offered coaching for female entrepreneurs. Giadha says she noticed there was a generational identity crisis among many of her clients caused by a conflict between new opportunities and traditional expectations.

"I come from a traditional Italian/Cuban family. And upon moving to the US, I realized that I was not happy with what they had planned for me: to get married to a wealthy gentleman, be the perfect wife and mother, and never have to work a day in my life," Giadha says. "It is no longer clear what our gender roles are. We are no longer raised to be moms and wives, but we are still expected to be both by society and our parents' and grandparents' generation. We are now also expected to be breadwinners and economic contributors, yet it is unclear how that would impact our ability to manage love and family. So, in essence, we are expected to be everything."

The result, she says, is many women finding themselves resentful for "having to be something we are not" and feeling pressure "from both men and some older women to be strong, unemotional, and to some degree 'pay our dues.'"

She admits the concept—can we really succeed in love and business?—was a "quirky experiment" and the execution of it was challenging. "I was going to launch a business on camera, truthfully, in public, showing women what it takes, and at the same time, I was going to try and succeed in life. I was going to work with a matchmaker and do everything available to a twenty-first-century, single woman. I was going to unveil the good, the bad, and the ugly."

The series followed Giadha suffering through awkward lunches and dinners, navigating match.com and PinkCupid, and enduring blind dates. At the end of 90 days, she had indeed successfully started New Frontier, and she also found love, but not in the way she anticipated. "Ironically, not at all from any of the dates. I ended up falling in love with the cinematographer that was following me around, so go figure," she laughs.

Looking forward, Giadha believes New Frontier has only begun to tap its potential for the cannabis industry as more states line up to legalize medicinal and adult recreational use, which will create an onslaught of new data to analyze. "We've been positioning for a while, so we are very ready," she says. "This moment is definitely happening faster than we thought, but this is exactly the type of culmination that we were hoping for. Investors across the country are looking for answers on how best to move forward in this blossoming industry.

New Frontier is the only firm currently collecting and aggregating the various data sets necessary to provide comprehensive and factual answers. Because of the colorful nature of this industry, we spend a great deal of time ensuring the data and data sources are vetted before we ingest or analyze any information. We like to say we're agnostic," she adds. "We're not for or against marijuana legalization. We're just trying to vet and provide the best data on this growing industry as quickly as possible."

The ultimate goal, Giadha says, is to project and understand the dynamic driving the industry. "Early on we saw that recreational adult use sales were driving the rest of the industry and making up a large portion of the growth sales. However, we anticipate that by 2020 when we look at adult use versus medical use, medical is likely to encompass the largest portions of those sells. Then after that, hemp will likely obliterate gross medical and recreational growth sales in the long run because of the plant's versatility and cost effectiveness. You can also use it to build beams for high-rises as well as bacteria-free textiles for the healthcare industry. It is just insanely versatile."

The upshot: now is the time for other entrepreneurs, especially women, to consider entering the cannabis industry.

"I found opportunities here through an entrepreneurial journey I wouldn't have had in any other place. If I can do it, you all can do it."

OAKSTERDAM UNIVERSITY

It was a scene straight out of a TV cop show, except this time, the bullets and the fear was real. On April 2, 2012, agents from the U.S. Marshals Service, the Drug Enforcement Agency, and the Internal Revenue Service—armed with a battering ram, a sledgehammer, power saws and a locksmith—conducted a coordinated raid. Their targets were Oaksterdam University, the home of cannabis activist and Oaksterdam founder Richard Lee, a medical cannabis dispensary called Coffeeshop Blue Sky, the Oaksterdam Museum, and storage space rented by K Seymour, the university's parent company. Many of the agents were masked and armed.

The government agents seized most of the university's property and assets including business documents, files, a safe, bags of medical marijuana, computers, and dozens of marijuana plants. As news of the raid spread throughout the tight-knit community, hundreds of protesters assembled in downtown Oakland, many openly smoking marijuana.

Although the sale and use of medical marijuana had been legal in California since voters passed Proposition 215—the Compassionate Use Act of 1996—it remained designated a Schedule I drug by the Federal Drug Administration. The state-federal disconnect made for an uneasy coexistence that imploded that April morning.

At the time, the university's executive chancellor Dale Sky Jones—who called the raid an attack on regulation—admitted the raid had decimated Oaksterdam. "It was one of the most damaging things that could happen to a business. Almost like a fire or a flood. Except this was an act of the federal government, not an act of God or nature."

Oaksterdam instructor and criminal defense lawyer Kali Grech says. "We knew it would never be the same again. There was a lot of great fear in a lot of people's lives. They could prosecute everyone; they could prosecute no one. It's also a scar. We remember back to that time as being very painful."

None if the government agencies that participated in the raid ever provided an official explanation. And no charges were ever filed. But the ramifications reverberated through the California cannabis community. Although the university survived, their post-raid operation was much smaller and in a new location. It put a chill on investment into the cannabis industry. And it prompted Lee— who was briefly detained and questioned at his apartment during the raid—to step away from his brainchild.

When announcing his resignation, he said, "I've been doing this for a long time. Over twenty years. I kind of feel like I've done my time. It's time for others to take over, partly to keep my legal issues separate so that Oaksterdam University can go on without problems." But stepping away from Oaksterdam didn't mean giving up softening his stance. "I believe that cannabis prohibition is unjust and counterproductive. What I've done is ethical, and I tried to use the resources that I had to do everything I could to change the laws."

The seeds of activism that would culminate in the founding of the first cannabis trade school in the United States were sown in the aftermath of a terrible accident. In the 1980s, the Texas native was working as a roadie lighting technician. While preparing for an Aerosmith concert in New Jersey, Lee fell from a catwalk and suffered a catastrophic spinal injury that left him paralyzed from the waist down. He started self-medicating with marijuana to ease chronic back spasms.

A year after his accident, Lee was carjacked in Houston. He would later tell the *San Francisco Chronicle* that it took police more than an hour to respond—a symptom, he believed, of law enforcement's preoccupation with arresting marijuana dealers rather than cracking down on violent crime.

"I felt like, here was this wonderful medicine of cannabis that had helped me so much, and why were the cops going after people using and selling it instead of the psychos and sociopaths who are out there robbing people? I thought I should do something about it."

Lee started his activism in 1992 by opening a hemp products store in Houston called Legal Marijuana. He also began advocating for pot legalization, finding inspiration in marijuana activist Dennis Peron. "I had to find a new career, and I found it in cannabis politics."

In 1997, after California decriminalized medical use marijuana, Lee moved to Oakland and co-founded the Hemp Research Center, which provided medical cannabis through the Oakland Cannabis Buyers Club. (Jim McClelland, a founding member of the club, is credited with coining the name *Oaksterdam*—a combination of Oakland and the very cannabis-friendly Amsterdam—to describe the neighborhood where the cannabis business first blossomed.) The center also researched horticultural methods to cultivate marijuana.

In 1999, Lee opened another dispensary, the Bulldog Coffeeshop, and in 2003 he formed the Oakland Civil Liberties Alliance, a political action committee that helped pass Oakland's Measure Z, which made private sales, cultivation, and possession of cannabis the lowest priority for law enforcement. The measure also mandated that Oakland tax and regulate cannabis as soon as possible under state law.

From 2005 to 2007, Lee published the *Oaksterdam News*, a quarterly newspaper with a circulation of over 100,000. During that time, he also funded the creation of *West Coast Cannabis* magazine and managed businesses including the Oaksterdam Gift Shop and Nursery. Then, on a trip to Amsterdam in 2006, where it is just as easy to buy cannabis as it is coffee, Lee says he was inspired to educate people about cannabis in a more formal environment.

"They had a kind of activists' operation there called the Cannabis College. It was a little grow place set up next to one of the big seed stores, and people would come in and give advice about growing."

Lee reimagined the idea into Oaksterdam University, a private trade school that would train and educate would-be entrepreneurs on how to start a business in California's medical marijuana industry. Rather than focusing solely on horticulture, Lee designed a more comprehensive curriculum that included all aspects of the plant such as politics, Patient relations, economics, legal issues, concentrates, and even cooking. The university's unique course study generated massive media attention here and abroad.

The first class in the fall of 2007 consisted of twenty students crammed into a small classroom, and their instructors included some of the biggest names in the cannabis industry of the time. Through word of mouth, interest exploded. Less than a year later, Lee opened a satellite campus in Los Angeles. After Michigan passed its medical cannabis law, Oaksterdam University offered to bring its services to Ann Arbor for a weekend seminar. Once again, the response was overwhelming, and people wanting to reserve a seat barraged the school with phone calls. Oaksterdam held the first Michigan class in May 2009 then later opened another satellite office in Flint, Michigan.

In 2009 the university moved to a 30,000-square-foot campus that offered roomier classrooms, auditoriums, and a state-of-the-art grow lab. As class sizes grew to 54 students, class frequency also increased. Instead of only holding classes on the weekend, Oaksterdam began offering semester-length classes on weekday evenings. That same year, the university started holding seminars in Michigan, Nevada, Colorado, and Washington DC—all places where medical marijuana was legal.

At its peak, Oaksterdam University had several hundred students, a hundred instructors, and a three-month waiting list for enrollment. In 2010 Lee said, "We're bringing in lots of students from all over the country, so that's good for the city, selling lots of hotel rooms and other business. We have about a hundred students in our weekend seminars that we hold a couple of times per month, and then we have a few hundred students enrolled in our semester programs at any one time. We have three semesters a year, so we're over 12,000 now for the first three years."

But the University's success also attracted the attention of federal authorities. "One of the things that made the feds mad was we had a nursery," Lee later said. "We sold cuttings."

It also didn't help that in 2010 Lee had gained global notoriety for writing Prop 19, the California ballot initiative to legalize adult use. Lee had drafted Prop. 19 despite opposition from some other legalization activists who argued it wasn't the best time to push for recreation use because mid-term elections have smaller voter turnouts. Others thought it didn't go far enough because it would only legalize possession and personal cultivation; cities and counties would decide whether to regulate and tax commercial growth— or even to allow it at all. Critics of the initiative believed the only way to convince the public to legalize cannabis was through a mandated, statewide regulatory model—like how alcohol is sold and controlled—with the state collecting taxes.

Lee followed his gut and spent more than $1.45 million of his companies' money to promote Prop. 19. His reasoning was simple. "I think the issue can't wait. We've been proven right that the campaign has made this a legitimate political issue."

When asked by a prescient reporter if he was concerned, should

Prop 19 pass, that federal law enforcement would try to shut it down, Lee downplayed the risk. "I think it'll most likely be similar to the history of Prop. 215 where the feds did come in and harass and bust a few people, but in the long run they're losing the war, and here we are 14 years later, and they haven't been able to stop that either. I think there's going to be a lot of hope given to a lot of people out there that laws are going to change around the rest of the country, just because historically things have started in California, just like they did with medical marijuana, and a lot of other social rights issues."

Prop 19 failed, and eighteen months later Oaksterdam was raided in a flex of federal muscle. OU's provost and dean, Aseem Sappal, believes it was a purely political move designed to temper Californians support for legalizing recreational use. "We got raided by federal authorities because of our support for Proposition 19 in California. The first effort to legalize recreational use failed in 2010. The feds knew we were going to push again in 2012 and that it had a strong chance of being enacted. So, we got raided."

To protect the university. Lee decided to step down as president—he was replaced by Dale Sky Jones—and cut off all involvement with the school and its related businesses. Lee later admitted he was worried the Feds would file major drug charges against him. Even though it was a risk he lived with and accepted for many years, the raid brought a different perspective.

"I never wanted to be the 'leader' of the legalization movement. I saw myself as just one small soldier in a big war. But I look at it as a battlefield promotion."

He eventually transferred his dispensary to new operators and shut down his nursery because the federal agents had confiscated his stock of mother plants, which he had nurtured for years. Since resigning from the university, Lee has worked with his mother, Ann, who founded Republicans Against Marijuana Prohibition in 2012.

Although Oaksterdam never closed, it lost its lease and had to leave its three-story citadel and relocate to a much smaller storefront across the street, where it also hosts the Cannabis Museum. Staffing was also slashed, and enrollment dropped off sharply after the raid thanks to the legal cloud left in its wake. Practically speaking, Jones was starting the university over from scratch and focused on keeping Oaksterdam open as a school even if it was no longer a dispensary. It was a nervous time for students, instructors, and administrators alike.

A year after the raid, Jones said, "It's been probably the most intense period of my life. "The ship was just upside down. We had just been gutted. All our properties were raided, and everything was taken, so we did have to downsize. Getting the ship righted and realizing you have no tools, no rigging, most of your crew is lost at sea, and there's no actual guarantee you will even find dry land—

you just keep swimming."

Oaksterdam University was deeply wounded by the raid. But it survived to teach another day—and train the next generation of cannabis-related business owners who will reap the rewards of activists like Lee as an increasing number of states legalize marijuana use—despite the FDA's refusal to reclassify cannabis, which seems based more on politics than medical science.

And the economic benefits of legalized cannabis are difficult to ignore. A 2010 OaklandNorth report noted:

> In 2004, the city granted permits to four licensed dispensaries, which quickly generated upwards of $17 million in just three years of business. Five years [after Measure Z passed], nearly 80 percent of Oakland's voters approved Measure F, authorizing the city to impose a 1.8 percent tax on all cannabis business activity—the first tax of its kind in the nation. At the time of the 2009 local ballot measure election, the city estimated that Measure F would raise roughly $294,000 in additional tax revenue in 2010.
>
> Supporters also say the dispensaries, many of which are located along the Broadway corridor, helped revitalize downtown Oakland by generating business

and much-needed foot traffic. "Before the dispensaries took off, the neighborhoods surrounding Harborside and Oaksterdam were lackluster and downtrodden," [Steve] D'Angelo said. Now, "Not only do we have world-class restaurants, but we also have two world-class theaters. You go downtown on weekends now, and there are people, there's activity, and none of that was happening before medical cannabis was licensed in the city of Oakland.

Fast forward to 2014. Oaksterdam is once again selling out its courses, with students—especially baby boomers—willing to pay $700 for a four-day intensive course in cultivation. Sappal, the university dean, wants to build Oaksterdam's credibility as a serious institution of higher learning.

"We have high school grads sitting next to oncologists and city council members. We have senators, governors, former congressmen—this is who we're working with. We have skepticism because it's a big joke, people just smoking pot. But the country is moving in this direction for a reason."

In addition to what they learn, for many OU students there is equal value in who you meet. "You have no idea how many people come here and end up going into partnership with someone they meet," Sappal says. "If there's a student in a class of 50 who's an electrician, that's a tremendous opportunity for networking. Because when you have an indoor grow, who's going to set it up? You want someone who's friendly. Some people may disagree with cannabis, but the bottom line is that the laws are changing, and the American people are speaking. If you're going to give them the keys to the car, you need to give them driver's ed."

As the industry matures, OU's certification program carries more weight with cannabis employers. As the website notes: "If you are applying for a job at a dispensary, our hope is that our certification program will give you the advantage in the selection process over someone who has not received certification. Certification shows that you have taken all our courses and have proved that you have met our standards of knowledge in the cannabis industry. Once receiving certification from us, you are encouraged to list Oaksterdam University under *special training*. Dispensaries can then call and verify that you are a student in good standing."

Students have a variety of reasons for wanting to immerse themselves in cannabis education. Some are activists who want to be more fully informed. Some focus on special interests so they can reach a wider audience by writing books. Some want to learn more about controlling chronic pain and growing their own plants. And some are budding entrepreneurs who are looking to start a business either through establishing their own commercial kitchens, grow rooms, dispensaries, or other cannabis-related enterprises.

Jeff Jones, Dale Sky Jones's husband, who runs the Patient ID Center, notes that California's medical marijuana law was driven in part because of the HIV/AIDS crisis and the need to ease suffering. Jones says that while HIV is no longer a driver, "You have a lot of baby boomers that are in pain who want some alternative [to prescription drugs]. And this is a great alternative, especially when you are looking at it in a non-smoked form."

Like many activists, Jones envisions a two-track market between medical and recreational. On the one hand, the medical market, "will shrink to a small contingent of patients who need it and are likely going to be covered and supported by insurance and by their doctors, because it will be cheaper than other conventional therapies." On the other hand, "you're going to see the adult-use recreational track, which will pay for everything."

The support for legalized marijuana continues to grow throughout the United States and around the world, with countries from Jamaica to Uruguay decriminalizing or legalizing cannabis use. Interest in all things cannabis has never been higher, which is why Oaksterdam University continues to prosper and expand with traveling educational seminars and satellite campuses across the country—and potentially beyond.

OU's Sappal says, "I was contacted by some people in Jamaica about teaching them to grow marijuana without pesticides. We might open our first international satellite campus there."

As always, Oaksterdam University seeks to educate so cannabis can reach its full wellness potential. "The general community has a lack of education on the issue," Sappal says. "For instance, they don't know the different ways it's possible to ingest marijuana. People associate the word marijuana with smoking. But cannabis can be administered as a topical application, a capsule, or a vapor you inhale. To enter the blood stream faster, you could apply a tincture under the tongue.

"I often remind my students about the difference between being educated and opinionated. Oaksterdam educates. I'm an advocate of education. In our classes, we have students, next to CPAs, next to doctors and grandmothers."

Oaksterdam also remains a monument for and a reminder of every activist who worked to change public perceptions and promote the medical, emotional, social, and economic benefits of cannabis.

"There was once a Just Say No campaign, which was brilliant," Sappal says. "Now we have a Just Say Yes campaign. In ten years, I see all fifty states making it legal."

US HEMP WHOLESALE

Many cannabis entrepreneurs get into the industry because they see it as a great business opportunity. For US Hemp Wholesale founder Jeff Gallagher, there's a more personal connection. In 2006—as a single, widowed parent—he started having panic attacks and soon found himself on the merry-go-round of prescription medication.

"They gave me mood stabilizers and buffers for my stomach and Ambien to sleep and the next thing I know, I am on five different pharmaceuticals. I came across a guy who said he had made some capsules that would help with my anxiety. Long story short, Michigan had enacted a medical marijuana law, and he was taking the waste products, the stalks, and making them into an extract that he put in capsules." While industrial hemp is *Cannabis sativa*, it is not psychotropic like marijuana. "I thought: *Yeah, whatever*, but I tried them. What did I have to lose? I was already not feeling like myself."

Cannabis wasn't the first natural solution that Jeff tried, but it

179

was the last. Almost immediately he stopped having panic attacks and didn't feel the need to take his Xanax anymore. At first, Jeff suspected he was experiencing a placebo effect. "I hadn't taken a Xanax in two weeks and was thinking: *This is crazy. What's going on? It's all in my head.*"

But when he stopped taking the capsules, his anxiety came roaring back, so he went on a mission to see precisely what was in those capsules. Through his research, he discovered the active ingredient was a very high percentage of cannabidiol (CBD).

"So in 2012 I founded a company in Colorado with a brand called Dixie Botanicals that were industrial hemp-based CBD products manufactured at the time by a company called Red Dice Holdings," which is produced by another manufacturer, and US Hemp Wholesale does not carry this brand. "I bought a tincture from them that worked just as well as the capsules—and it wasn't made in a basement like the capsules were. Long story short, my anxiety was gone, and I had worked my way off all my medication. I was on zero pharmaceuticals. And I thought: *You know what? I want to help just five people a month with their anxiety.*"

Jeff started a now-defunct website called anxietynowwhat.com.

"It was a big flop," he laughs. "But I started my little company in May 2013 and put some products on Amazon and eBay and was selling five bottles a month. That was my goal: five. It was really just a hobby."

Until neurosurgeon and CNN medical correspondent, Sanjay Gupta, appeared in a documentary in August 2013 about marijuana called *Weed* and extolled the benefits of cannabidiol.

"He said CBD was great for a whole bunch of issues," Jeff recalls. "Well, at that time there were maybe two CBD sellers in the entire country: me and the people I'm buying it from, Dixie Botanicals. If you had Googled CBD back then, I was number one in the search rankings. And that's when it all just skyrocketed. I went from selling five bottles a month to almost a hundred bottles a day. All I was doing every day and into the night was stuffing packages and shipping them out because it was just me. So that's how my business got started from a hobby."

Before becoming a cannabis entrepreneur, Jeff had worked in IT most of his adult life as a network engineer systems administrator, doing larger scale assignments of servers. "I was doing cloud computing before cloud computing was cool," he jokes. "I was self-employed and used to work from my basement doing IT work."

Jeff says he's always been an entrepreneur; it's in his blood. "My grandmother owned a baseball card shop, and I've been in several business ventures. I part-owned a construction company; I did house remodeling. I was even a landlord for a minute. So a lot of that has helped me in the business world."

Like many in Michigan, the Great Recession hit Jeff hard in 2009. "I lost my really good, high-paying job and couldn't find work for two years. I went back to business school, took some classes, and started a company pretty much from nothing. I got screwed over and walked away from my business partner in June 2012. I had to start over from zero and swore I'd never have another partner. And I haven't. I own 100 percent of US Hemp Wholesale and am debt-free."

Since Gupta's documentary aired on CNN, Jeff's hobby has grown to a seven-figure business, generating more than $1.7 million in 2015 and is on track to beat that in 2016. But running a cannabis-based business is much more complicated than the IT world.

"This market has changed many times," he sighs. "When I got into it there was one other player and me, and now there are three hundred players in this space, and more than half of them buy from me in some capacity. Hemp has to be imported to be legal for commerce[1] and so I still import from Europe; although I hope to have hemp in the ground in Michigan soon."

---

[1] In the Federal Farm Bill of 2014, the 7606 provision allows hemp to be grown for agricultural or academic research.

Jeff also has to navigate the complexities created by federal law that is out of sync with state law. For example, the Federal Drug Administration (FDA) has deemed CBD a drug as opposed to a supplement and sent a letter to Jeff and seven other companies saying he was marketing an unapproved drug. The background to the letter is indicative of the regulatory maze facing cannabis entrepreneurs. The FDA determined that we couldn't market products based on (CBD) as dietary supplements because of a pre-existing investigational new drug (IND) filing on the compound by GW Pharmaceuticals. According to regulation, an ingredient that is the subject of an IND cannot be marketed in supplements.

However, there is an exception if the ingredient was already marketed as a supplement or food before the filing of the IND. Cannabis activists argue that to restrict CBD from being sold as a dietary supplement; there had to be thorough investigations by GW Pharmaceuticals that *were made public* before those sales. They contend the public aspect didn't happen until late 2013, well after several companies had already started selling CBD. Even so, nobody can be sure how the FDA will ultimately rule. Jeff is not optimistic.

"GW Pharmaceuticals filed for the IND status for CBD and THC and paid the FDA for each. My company and every other company in the hemp-based CBD space has paid the FDA zero. So who's back is the FDA going to have? It ain't going to be mine," he chuckles. "It's going to be the guy who gave them a check. So the whole industry is shifting again. I don't sell CBD anymore; I sell food and dietary supplements with whole-plant hemp extract with its natural constituents, which has been marketed since the mid-twentieth century as a dietary supplement. The whole market has begun to shift to this position. The end result will probably be consumer confusion, which is unfortunate. The last thing I want is to confuse further the people that I am trying to educate."

The uncertainty has also affected hemp entrepreneurs' banking abilities. "When I started out, my local bank gave me a merchant account.

Hemp? You're not smoking it, right?
It's food.
Oh, yeah, that's perfect. Sure!

"They were fine with it. Then CBD got popular, and all of a sudden it was an unapproved category with merchant accounts. Everybody in this market has started using an international processing company because they can't get a domestic one—again, making it harder on the consumer. But it's working."

The growing number of states legalizing marijuana for medical and recreational use reflects the changing public views on cannabis. The demonization of cannabis resulted in, among other consequences, federal restrictions on growing hemp plants for any reason.

"For sure the perception of hemp is changing a lot," Jeff says. "Even the perception of marijuana is changing. I'm in the helping people business."

Jeff's focus is to promote the nutritional and health benefits of industrial hemp. "We hear amazing stories about how the products are changing the lives of people all over the world. That's where I feel good about doing what I do. I donate to all kinds of local children's charities and foundations; that's where my heart is at."

However, Jeff stresses, "I am not a doctor, and I do not want to misrepresent what hemp can do for people. We do not make any claims or insinuate that our products can treat, cure, prevent, or mitigate any health condition."

Jeff explains he is a licensed, wholesale food processor with the State of Michigan and follows good manufacturing practices (GMP), which refers to a system of manufacturing that guarantees reproducibility of product quality to set specifications. "Everything I do is considered food, except our vape line. But it is all food-grade ingredients; technically you could eat it—which we do not recommend as the flavor is very strong—but you can also vape it."

But his heart is with research, and that is what he spends most of his energy trying to realize. "Part of that is trying to get the doctors on board and not having the hospitals freak out and say: *But it's pot.*"

For now, Jeff is working in the industrial hemp space. "My wife doesn't want me in the marijuana game in Michigan," he admits, "because it's still illegal at a federal level."

Jeff acknowledges education is a crucial responsibility for cannabis entrepreneurs. "In the space I'm in, there are a lot of hustlers selling junk, so 90 percent of what I do is education, 10 percent is selling. I have a dedicated staff, and we all love helping people. We're all in the helping people business. We all want to see people do better. Everything I sell is for the overall health and well-being of the human body."

Despite his emphasis on general wellness, current FDA rules make marketing his and all supplemental products tricky. "We can say positive things like *immune support, circulatory support,* and *helps brain function,* but by FDA rules we cannot say anything that changes a negative to a positive. All dietary supplements follow the same purview. If you look at any packaging on any dietary supplement, it'll say stuff like *supports, soothes, calms.* It doesn't say: *Fixes x.*"

Jeff's passion for helping people with hemp-based products goes deeper than his experience with anxiety relief. "The medical community misdiagnosed my late wife. They misdiagnosed her and then over-prescribed her, and she died," he says. "I blame the pharmaceutical companies for her death, period. End of discussion. And then I started becoming a pharmaceutical pill popper too because that was the way the game's rigged. You go to your doctor, they give you a pill, and then next thing you know: *Oh, you've got a stomach issue.* Now they give you another pill. And then the next thing you know, you got another issue, you can't sleep, and they give you another pill ... before you know it you're on all these pills, which don't go to the cause of the original problem."

Over the last several years Jeff has dedicated himself to learning all he can about cannabinoids. "I've been doing a lot of research. I have a network of researchers and other industry leaders who I work and share information with."

Raphael Mechoulam, sometimes called the father of medical marijuana research, is a University of Jerusalem chemist credited with isolating THC. According to Mechoulam, THC mimics compounds produced in our bodies called endogenous cannabinoids, which are part of what is called the endocannabinoid system (ECS). Cannabinoids help regulate the flow of neurotransmitters, so scientists suspect THC can either increase or decrease the flow of the neurotransmitters. In the '70s and '80s, Mechoulam published studies that showed CBD could curb seizures, research that the medical establishment largely ignored until recent years.

Also, different endocannabinoid receptors are found in non-nerve cells in the immune system, leading researchers to suspect cannabis may have broad medical implications, from helping fight cancer to treating concussions and Crohn's disease. Jeff believes it's an avenue researchers need to thoroughly investigate.

"I've read the patents. I've read the clinical research from Israel. I'm educated in the plant. I know enough about the plant that they could almost give me an honorary PhD in phytocannabinoids science because I've forgotten more than most people know now," he jokes. "The next phase for my company is putting in a full analytical lab to do heavy metals, pesticide, mold, and cannabinoid profiles internally because there's a bunch of domestic hemp coming, so I want to be ready for that. And if Michigan passes the law, they're going to need analytics labs to do all the marijuana testing to prove the quality and for the THC sites to use. So I'm not going to grow it, but I'll test it."

The planned facility is ambitious, covering four thousand square feet. "We're negotiating to grow industrial hemp in partnership with a local university. I have farmers who also want to partner with me for research. I tell all these people we could probably cover their fuel costs to plant it, but that's about it."

Financial gain though doesn't seem to be the driving force behind the interest Jeff's venture is generating. "It's all volunteers;

it's all for research. I provide the seed, but you have to get it in the ground. So that's the next piece of my venture, while we'll continue to sell hemp extract all over the world."

The demand for hemp extracts is global, with US Hemp Wholesale servicing customers in South Africa, Europe, and Japan. New Canadian regulations now allow US companies to sell hemp extract there.

Jeff says his products are sought after because they are diligent about quality control, a vital element when buying from international suppliers. "I have people I know and trust personally walk the fields. I have three different sources in Europe," Jeff reports, adding that he does not buy from China because of quality control concerns.

The company website stresses that "all the supplements and nutritional products distributed by US Hemp Wholesale are laboratory tested by third parties to ensure purity, quality, and consistency—and that it is not marijuana. We retain the test results to prove it."

While he's happy with his current suppliers, Ideally, Jeff will eventually be able to buy home-grown US hemp once legislators and policy makers recognize the scientific, practical, medical, and economic value of hemp. "It's a rotation crop," he points out. "You don't grow it every year. So every farmer in the United States that grows anything would want to rotate hemp into their space."

But as with any cash crop, there's more to growing hemp than simply throwing some seeds on the ground. "For example, the hemp that's grown in Michigan can't be grown in California; because of the climate and the soil conditions you couple possibly get marijuana." Meaning it exceeds a certain level of THC, currently .3 percent. "For that matter, Southern California hemp probably can't be grown in Northern California either for the same reason. So we want to develop a certified strain of hemp for growing in Michigan's climate that will be below the THC levels, so we won't have to worry about it, and all is good."

That said, Jeff believes regulators need to raise the acceptable THC levels, explaining, "The higher the THC level, the stronger the fiber, so there's some back and forth on that issue."

Once he finalizes his university partnership, Jeff will look to come up with new avenues for research. "We're going for intellectual property on hemp, so I want to put five groups of graduate students/assistants together and have them all come up with ideas for one of 50,000 verticals that can be made with hemp—from plastics to batteries and beyond. I'll get a committee together, and we'll pick one idea for each group, and my company will invest money for those research projects and let the graduate students run with it.

We're going to fund it, and we're going to let them roll. Am I going to manufacture hemp concrete or plastic? Probably not. But I might own part of the intellectual property."

Jeff admits his relationship with hemp borders on the existential. "I love the plant, to be honest, and several people have told me that hemp picks who it wants to pick. I would never have picked it. It picked me. I didn't get into this to make money. I got into this to get off my Xanax. Now I have fourteen full-time employees, and I'm humbled by that every day."

WHOOPI & MAYA

From the fight for suffrage that began in the nineteenth century, to the feminist movement of the 1960s, to the current struggle to ensure equal pay for equal work, American women have been playing social, political, and cultural catch-up pretty much since the Mayflower dropped anchor. The same has been true with medical issues. The attitudes and biases that brought us female hysteria in the 1800s fuel efforts to run roughshod over women's reproductive rights in the new millennium, deny maternity leave, or simply ignore women-specific health issues altogether.

One of those seldom addressed conditions is menstrual pain. Other than daytime TV ads for Midol, the medical community has largely given a collective shrug to symptoms that afflict millions of women every month—including Whoopi Goldberg. "The only products available to us," she says, "were filled with ingredients we couldn't even pronounce. If men got cramps, this problem would have been solved a long time ago."

193

To emphasize that point, she notes that when she first asked if anyone in the cannabis space was targeting menstrual cramps, the answer was no. "I was told it would be a 'niche' product. But how can half the population on earth be a niche market? That seems to be people flippantly blowing you off, which is what you get whenever you start talking about cramps. They weren't thinking: *How do you target this?* I have grown granddaughters who have severe cramps, so I said this is what I want to work on."

Taking a proactive approach, Whoopi took matters into her own entrepreneurial hands. Partnering with award-winning edibles creator Maya Elisabeth, they have developed a line of non-smoking medical-cannabis products to alleviate menstrual pain. "This was all inspired by my own experience from a lifetime of difficult periods," Whoopi says. "And the fact that cannabis was literally the only thing that gave me relief."

Maya explains why cannabis is so effective. "CBD is very helpful for inflammation and pain and THC is also very helpful for pain. Combined with other superfoods and medicinal herbs, it can provide the type of relief many women need. It also elevates your mood and relaxes your mind so that your body can do what's it's supposed to do, which is feel comfortable and heal. It's honestly the wonder, miracle medicine."

While it might not have exactly taken a village, Whoopi's

journey to cannabis business owner crossed paths with others in the industry, such as the owner of Alternative Herbal Health Services (AHHS). In 2004 Dina Browner—known affectionately as Dr. Dina by her numerous West Hollywood, CA, clients—became the first woman to open a regulated medical marijuana dispensary in Southern California. She is not a medical doctor, but over the years she has become a well-known activist and medical-cannabis consultant, touting the myriad health and wellness benefits of cannabis.

Dina herself ended up in the cannabis industry through sheer serendipity. In 2002 a friend with stage III testicular cancer called her, suicidal over the chemotherapy side effects and his inability to keep any food or medicine down. Dina brought over a joint, and almost immediately his nausea eased, his appetite increased, and his outlook brightened. The downside: even though California legalized medical marijuana in 1996, getting a prescription from a doctor wasn't easy for the average person.

Dina found a Northern California doctor willing to write her friend a prescription for cannabis. She drove her friend to San Francisco to meet with the doctor. By the time they left, the doctor had agreed to make a weekly trip to see Los Angeles patients if Dina agreed to run the office. That solved half the problem. The other issue back then was finding a place to utilize their prescriptions.

Dina says, "At that point, I realized we had a need for dispensaries. So, I talked to a couple of friends who decided to open a dispensary in West Hollywood."

AHHS is still there and still growing, as is Dina's reputation as a highly-regarded dispensary consultant. Over time the dispensary has developed an A-list clientele comprised of entertainer, actors, and even politicians. One of those clients was Whoopi. A profile in *Forbes* notes, "Whoopi Goldberg visited AHHS and was enamored. The two ladies discovered their shared ideals about treating debilitating diseases. Whoopi fell in love with the idea of medicinal marijuana aiding menstrual cramps. Advils simply did not work."

Dina explains, "Most women don't feel comfortable walking into a male-centric dispensary, so when they do and ask for a solution, they simply ask for pain relief, rather than menstrual pain relief. It is a product needed 12 times a year."

Enter Maya, the founder of Om Edibles, an all-female cannabis collective in Northern California established in 2008. To hear her talk, working in the cannabis industry was kismet.

"It all started out with a deep love for cannabis. And every single thing that I've done in life has been brought back to cannabis for me. After I graduated from San Francisco State with a degree in psychology, I got a job working in a dispensary for a few years, and

I got the opportunity to serve thousands of patients with cannabis medicine in all different forms and started to observe so many cannabis miracles. I was able to connect with each person, ask what everyone's goals were, what their intentions and needs were, and take the time to educate them about cannabis, about which strains worked well for what. It was during that time I put my first edible on the shelf. It was a frozen cookie dough."

By the time the dispensary shut down, Maya says she had "caught the bug and started my own edible company in 2008, making truffles with my best friend." On the Whoopi & Maya website, she calls it perfect timing "because it was full trim season, and after months of work I got together enough earnings to do my own grow and make edibles at the same time."

They called the startup Queen 215, a nod toward Proposition 215, the California ballot initiative that made medical marijuana legal. "I ended up moving from there to a point where I was just relying on edibles, and now it's become something where even if I wanted to do something else, I wouldn't have the time. People like the products and keep wanting them, and this is what I'll do. It's an awesome feeling."

In 2012 they renamed the company Om Edibles, which is now known for creating high- quality edibles, tinctures, and topicals—about 30 products—all from their own cannabis strains.

The company has also received a lot of ink for being an all-female growing collective. But Maya says, "We never set out to be a female collective. We're just a lot of women who are passionate about cannabis. We're all good friends, and it was a natural evolution."

Maya says an integral aspect of the company's growth was entering various competitions. "We ended up winning some awards for some of our original creations—we won our first High

Times' Cannabis Cup in 2012, and in 2015 we earned six more awards between US and Jamaican Cups." Those competitions also played a big role in leading Whoopi to her collective's kitchen doorstep.

When Whoopi had the idea to develop cannabis products for menstrual pain, she called Rick Cusick of *High Times*. "He remembered that we were a female collective who had some awards," Maya says. "He reached out to us and asked if we'd be the group of women to talk to about this. I said: *Yes, absolutely*. It was totally a surprise and something I never saw coming. From there I reached out to my herbalist friend Alexis Gandara, and we started building the four products from there."

Whoopi serves as chairwoman, Maya is CEO, and the company is based in Northern California. A year after forming their partnership, the company launched its first products in April 2016. The Signature

Line included a raw sipping chocolate infused with either CBD or THC, a topical rub for localized pain, THC-infused tincture designed for serious discomfort, and relaxing THC-infused bath soak. The products come in several scents, sizes, and strengths and can be used separately or together.

Maya designed each product for maximum effectiveness. For example, on the company website she explains that their topical is unique because "it has healing herbs in it aside from cannabis. It has an herb called Cramp Bark, which is named that because it's so helpful for period cramps. There are herbs that are good for hemorrhaging and mood elevation, and it contains nervines, which calm your nerves. Topicals have an incredible ability—when combined with the proper carrier oils—to go deep and penetrate your system. Studies have found that cannabis topically can help treat things like endocarditis. We do a proprietary blend of carrier oils that are also health beneficial and carry the medicine deep within your body."

She says the tincture includes a special blend of herbs like raspberry leaf and superfoods like elderberries. "Elderberries are delicious, they're beautifully bright and purple in color, and they're full of antioxidants and immune strengtheners. Besides being delicious, raw honey has antibiotic-like effects as well and is a natural preservative. Natural glycerin as part of our base means no harsh alcohol taste."

Maya describes their chocolate as "delicious, divine, raw, and organic. Raw cacao before it's processed, is the highest antioxidant-containing food on the planet, and it releases a whole slew of comfort hormones and happiness hormones, so it has nice soothing effects on the system."

Finally, the bath uses aromatherapy to intensify its relaxation benefits and help with alleviating PMS and general aches and pains. "The lavender calms your entire nervous system, the heat in the water makes your body release melatonin, which makes you tired, and the magnesium in the salts draw the toxins out, the ones that make you sore. I think these baths are in a category of their own. A topical affects you locally, an edible affects and alters your whole system, and this is doing both. It's not getting your head high, but it's relaxing you, taking away anxiety, and the effect on the body is super."

From Dina's perspective, "Whoopi and Maya have just made the Levis of today, a staple item that will last forever. There is zero competition for their product, not one single cannabis product for menstrual cramps is on the market." She also notes women will want to try it because "Whoopi is in a different category of trust for the consumer."

"It seems to be going very well," Maya reports. "We have a solid production team and sales staff, we've gotten amazing feedback, and it's just been moving right along. I just want people to find relief from our products and for word to get out there of what we're doing so people can have access to our medicine safely."

Whoopi muses that she sees cannabis "as a step in the direction of new forms of medicine, but it also has its place in history and goes back to Queen Victoria. There are many people trying to get you high; this is a product specifically just to get you comfortable. Smoking a joint is fine, but most people can't smoke a joint and go to work. This, you can put it in your purse. You can put the rub on your lower stomach and lower back at work, and then when you get home you can get in the tub for a soak or make tea, and it allows you to continue to work throughout the day. What I'm hoping is that if enough women find relief through cannabis, they will become more empathetic to other medical marijuana users, including families who are moving their children to places where it's legal so they can get what they need to feel better."

While she may be a newcomer to the cannabis industry, Whoopi has long spoken of using marijuana to ease severe headaches associated with her glaucoma. In a column for *The Cannabist* blog, she extolled the virtues of vaping. "I took a sip. It was beautiful. And my pen and I have been together ever since. The vape pen has changed my life. With each sip comes relief— from pressure, pain, stress, discomfort."

201

The reality is there's scant scientific research available about the medical benefits of cannabis primarily because the federal government has severely restricted it. Only now are trials ongoing to study its potential benefits for PTSD and seizure. But a lack of published research doesn't mean there isn't a trove of anecdotal evidence. In a *Daily Beast* interview, Whoopi dismissed suggestions that using cannabis for menstrual cramps hasn't been studied enough to pursue.

"How can you have a male expert tell any woman what works for her period? Just because they haven't done the studies does not mean women haven't been finding relief wherever they can. I can't say that every woman will find relief from our product, but the ones that do will be better for it. I want women to know that there might be a solution that will change their lives in a positive way. Again, I'm not advocating getting anybody high. I'm advocating a better quality of life. I've gotten older, and I want to help people feel better—that's my groove."

Well, one of her grooves. In a press release distributed after the product launch, Whoopi noted that the company's mandate goes beyond just providing an effective product, but also to educating the public and supporting social reform. To that end, Whoopi argues on her *Cannabist* blog that there is a need to include menstrual pain as well as other conditions under the medical cannabis umbrella everywhere. After New York State announced that only a short list of conditions would qualify for medical marijuana, she wrote:

I'm sorry to say the governor's plan doesn't include conditions like glaucoma, migraines or severe menstrual disorders—very real issues for people who suffer from them, myself included. I would have loved to have had a conversation with the governor and his staff. I'd tell him: *There are so many people this could help—and while a lot of people think others are champing at the bit to go out and party with medical marijuana, that's just not the case. People are desperate— really desperate—for the medication that helps them. And as we have seen, if we can't get it with your help here in New York, we end up having to go to other states.*

Whoopi also envisions a day when federal law will catch up to the growing public sentiment. "Where marijuana is a legitimate medicine and a brand-new industry that takes root in our cities and rural communities. Where farmers and gardeners will grow cannabis for those in medical need. Where doctors and budtenders work with [patients] by tracking progress, altering dosages and keeping watch. Where scientists [help] patients with professionally regularized doses to treat their conditions accurately. Those are important and very noble jobs and careers we should be excited about."

Until that brave new cannabis world arrives, Whoopi and Maya will continue trailblazing as public acceptance continues to grow. At the end of 2016 close to 30 states had passed medical marijuana laws and seven states plus Washington DC have also legalized adult recreational use, even though cannabis was still illegal on a federal level. Currently, because of state regulations, Whoopi & Maya products are only sold in California to those with a medical marijuana card.

The upside is that California is one of the world's largest cannabis markets. According to big data firm New Frontier, California generated $2.7 billion in sales in 2015, reflecting the large cannabis consumer base Whoopi & Maya products can reach. In the summer of 2016, California lawmakers approved several measures formalizing the state's medical marijuana system that provide the groundwork for a legal recreational system. Now that Prop 64 legalizing adult recreational use has passed, those measures could potentially give anyone offering medical marijuana products an advantage in selling recreational products, a prospect that will undoubtedly expand Maya & Whoopi's customer base.

But even before the passage of Prop 64, Maya believed their company was poised for success because they offer unique and effective products, are targeting an underserved market, and put a premium on quality.

"We are an ambitious company entering an ambitious industry," Maya says. "We can't wait to expand our product offerings and geographic reach." And she points out that their products aren't only for those with menstrual discomfort; many men would also find the products beneficial for easing other types of pain and promoting comfort and relaxation. "That's one of the things that's so beautiful about cannabis."

Beyond being the only company focused on menstrual pain, Whoopi and Maya themselves are a rarity in the cannabis industry. According to *USA Today*, "Another interest of the two women is in breaking what some are calling the *grass ceiling*—the limited participation of minorities and women in leadership roles in the cannabis industry. When it comes to starting marijuana-focused businesses, state regulators have written rules that tend to favor established small-business owners with access to capital and clean criminal records." In other words, white males.

In the same article, Maya notes that since marijuana remains illegal at the federal level, some would-be entrepreneurs shy away, wary after seeing how police and prosecutors disproportionally punish minorities when it comes to drug use. "A lot of white men don't have to think about this," she adds.

Maya offers this advice to the next generation of potential female cannabis entrepreneurs: "Choose something that you would like to see on the market that is health beneficial for patients and understand the responsibility that a lot of people you'll be serving have compromised immune systems or are truly turning to cannabis as an alternative medicine. So, remember every ingredient counts and try your best to produce the best quality products."

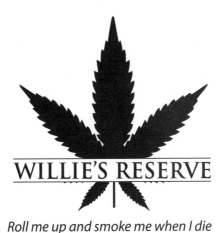

Roll me up and smoke me when I die
And if anyone don't like it, just look 'em in the eye
I didn't come here, and I ain't leavin'
So don't sit around and cry
Just roll me up and smoke me when I die.
(Willie Nelson, Kris Kristofferson, Snoop Dogg, Jamey Johnson)

Willie Nelson, one of the original outlaws of country music, has enjoyed a well-documented, sometimes notorious love affair with cannabis over the decades. And now he's mixing business with his long-time pleasure after launching his own cannabis brand for recreational users. Willie's Reserve sells buds of marijuana flower, pre-rolled joints, and cartridges of CO_2-extracted cannabis oil for vape pens through dispensaries. After rolling out in Colorado and Washington, the company plans on expanding as more states legalize recreational cannabis use.

The company website notes: "For decades, as Willie Nelson

and his band traveled from town to town, pot enthusiasts flocked to his shows. They happily shared the bounty from their home gardens and local communities. Now Willie's Reserve pays tribute to a tradition of sharing, caring, and toking. It's as if the Red-Headed Stranger has offered an invitation aboard the Honeysuckle Rose to sample the choicest selections of his stash."

A press release reports: "Consumers will be able to indulge with confidence, savoring each puff while knowing they're partaking in an age-old ritual that has bonded marijuana-lovers together since the first dried leaves were touched with flame."

Or as Willie says: "It's the best on the market. I will make sure it's good, or it won't be on sale. I don't like it when they put chemicals and pesticides in it. That makes it not much better than a regular old cigarette."

Willie appreciates marijuana the way oenophiles embrace their wine cellars—each serving is to be savored and appreciated for its unique notes. So, Willie's Reserve won't be restricted to one varietal; instead, the brand will offer several strains. "There are so many kinds of pot that do many different things," Willie says. "It's a good idea to have everything labeled for what it does, what it don't do, and how powerful it is."

While the financial potential of the venture is enormous, the new company will not stray far from Willie's entrenched social activism and populist roots—Willie's Reserve is committed to partnering with small, environmentally-sensitive farmers and cultivators.

"Now that legalization is spreading across the country, there's a great opportunity to build a company that can help a lot of people," Willie says. "I've smoked enough and I want to give back."

A Willie's Reserve spokesman adds, "This is a culmination of Willie's vision and his whole life."

By his accounts, cannabis has been a part of that life almost as long as music has. Born in the Central Texas town of Abbott in 1933, Willie says he grew up with an appreciation for music.

"I was raised and worked in the cotton fields around Abbott with a lot of African-Americans and a lot of Mexican-Americans, and we listened to their music all the time. I guess that's why I was influenced a lot by those around me; there was a lot of singing that went on in the cotton fields."

He got his first guitar when he was six and started writing songs not long after. While still in high school he performed with a local polka band and with a gospel group—his eclectic tastes evident even then. After graduating in 1950, Willie enlisted in the Air Force but was honorably discharged because of chronic back problems.

He enrolled in a farming program at Baylor University and made ends meet by working a series of odd jobs, including a door-to-door encyclopedia salesman.

His passion for music soon trumped his agriculture studies. He worked as a radio DJ and became a regular at local music clubs, performing original songs such as "Crazy" and "Funny How Time Slips Away." It was during that time when he smoked his first joint.

"I think I was probably 19 or 20 years old playing in bars in Fort Worth, and I ran into a guy who smoked pot, and I'd never smoked it before," Willie recalls. "I smoked for a long time without getting high. For months I would smoke and smoke, and I wasn't getting high, and I couldn't figure out why. And then one day I did, and I said, *Oh OK, that's what it's all about.*"

He moved to Nashville in 1960 and was hired by Pamper Music as a songwriter. Despite enjoying success writing hits for other performers, including Patsy Cline's legendary rendition of "Crazy," Willie was restless. His performing career was going nowhere. With his stylized delivery, roadhouse ambiance, and unique phrasing, Willie didn't fit the classic country mold of the early 1960s. His hard-living, hard-drinking, rough around the edges reputation made him that much more an outsider. That much more an outlaw.

His 1962 single "Touch Me" reached the country Top 10, but both

Willie's debut album, *And Then I Wrote,* and his second *Here's Willie Nelson* failed to chart. When his Tennessee home burned down in 1970, Willie took it as a sign from the universe that Nashville was not the place to be. He moved to Austin and immersed himself in the city's vibrant music scene, performing regularly at local venues.

Inspired by the social and music camaraderie of Woodstock, Willie organized and hosted Fourth of July picnics, which attracted other outlaw performers such as Kris Kristofferson and Waylon Jennings. (It remains a popular annual event.)

Unburdened by record producers trying to change his style and delivery, Willie flourished, recording his songs on his terms and earning him a small but devoted fan base. He released his third album, *Shotgun Willie* in 1973 was a critical success but chart disappointment, Ditto 1974's *Phases and Stages.*

Everything changed in 1975 with the release of *Red-Headed Stranger.* Finally, in his early 40s, Willie broke through. The album topped the country charts and crossed over to the pop Top 40. He also won his first Grammy for best country vocal performance.

In 1976 Willie joined Waylon Jennings, Jessi Colter, and Tompall Glaser on the compilation album, *Wanted! The Outlaws,* another critical and commercial success. He followed that up with the classic single "Mamas Don't Let Your Babies Grow Up to Be Cowboys," with

Jennings, which won the 1978 Grammy Award for best country vocal performance by a duo or group.

His music success led to Hollywood. In 1979 he appeared in *The Electric Horseman* opposite Robert Redford and Jane Fonda, and in 1980 starred as a country musician torn between his wife and a young singer in *Honeysuckle Rose.* The film was a modest box office success, but the song he wrote for it, "On the Road Again," earned Willie an Academy Award nomination for best original song and a Grammy Award for best country song. It also became his theme song.

Over his career Willie has recorded nearly 70 studio albums and sold more than 40 million. And he's still going, out on the road more than he's home, performing around 150 shows a year. And at each concert, he's greeted by fans who share his love of cannabis, and eager to share their best homegrown with him, and appreciate his advocacy efforts on behalf of their plant. While never overtly political, Willie has been a devout social activist for decades. In 1985 he, Neil Young, and John Mellencamp helped organize the first of many Farm Aid benefit concerts that have raised millions to help family farmers keep their land. Nelson is a vocal environmentalist, promoting alternative fuels and in 2004 started selling his own brand of biodiesel made from soybeans called BioWillie.

"It seems like that's good for the whole world if we can start growing our own fuel instead of starting wars over it," he says.

But for all his musical and film success, for all his social activism, it was his marijuana use—and arrests—that colored the public's perception of him.

In 1974, Willie was arrested in Dallas and charged with possession. In 1994, police in Waco busted Willie for having a joint. The arrest—and his mug shot—made the national news. The related court appearance also caused Willie to miss performing on the Grammys that year. In 2006 Willie and his sister were arrested in Louisiana and charged with possession after police found one and a half *pounds* of marijuana and three ounces of psychedelic mushrooms on his tour bus. The siblings pleaded guilty and were given a $1,024 fine and a six-month probation. And in 2010, he was arrested for having a relatively modest—for him—six ounces of marijuana in his tour bus while traveling from Los Angeles to Texas after Thanksgiving. He posted a $2,500 bond and was home before the turkey leftovers were gone.

And those are just the times that made the news. "I've been pulled over many times and busted many times, but I don't really remember the first one, it was so long ago," he admits.

While the legal consequences of his fondness for cannabis have been surprisingly minimal considering he lives in Texas, those experiences and his sense of social justice prompted Willie to become a staunch advocate for the decriminalization of cannabis, through his work with NORML (National Organization for the Reform of Marijuana Laws) and other groups. While part of the movement is prompted by the practical—to allow adults access to the plant if they want it—it is also a civil rights movement that seeks to end the disproportionate impact drug arrests have on poor communities and minorities.

Like many others, Willie says cannabis is safer and healthier than tobacco and alcohol. "I had emphysema, had all kinds of different health problems caused by drinking and smoking. I had a pack of Chesterfields, took them all out, threw them away, rolled up 20 big, fat numbers, stuck them into the Chesterfield pack, and I haven't smoked a cigarette since. And that's been 30, 40 years ago." But Willie says for him cannabis isn't just a vehicle to get high. "It has a lot to do with calming the nerves, which makes the creative juices flow a little easier. It's medicine, and it's already been proven to be medicine. End of story."

Willie isn't a teetotaler and admits to the occasional glass of wine. "I'm not afraid to take a drink of anything, but I just don't get a thrill from it. I don't need it."

He's also made the transition from paper joint to vape in deference to his voice. "I'm sure lighting up a joint is not that easy on your lungs. A singer has to think about stuff like that. Smoking a joint in paper is not as good for your lungs as it is doing it in a vaporizer. It's a no-brainer, really."

Willie admits he didn't initially appreciate edibles' different effect. "It's more of a body stone, I guess. It took me a little while to acclimate to it. I wasn't sure of it to begin with, but now it depends on what you want to do. If you want to go to sleep, eat a piece of candy, and you'll doze off."

What he's learned about cannabis over the years belies the misinformation Willie says he grew up hearing—in a nutshell, demon weed. Now research has found it is safer than alcohol and does not have the addictive qualities associated with tobacco cigarettes.

"It's not the only thing we've been lied to about, if you stop and think about it," Willie says, remembering being castigated and in some cases demonized for being a cannabis user. "I think we knew more than what most people gave us credit for knowing. We knew we're supposed to be bad people because we smoked marijuana, but we knew we weren't bad people. So, we knew somewhere in there was a discrepancy. People had to realize: *Wait a minute; it don't make him a bad guy just 'cause he smokes weed.*"

Willie told the Cannabist, "I'm still surprised it took this long for educated people to get a little sense. We've had so many negative things thrown at us about what it does to you and the bad things that marijuana can do to you. And *Reefer Madness* . . . that movie was horrible, and it made people really scared. And fear is a hard thing to overcome. So, all that had to be overcome. Now when people smoke or eat a piece of candy, they realize that: *What's the big deal?"*

Despite the dramatic shift in public opinion, Willie says there will also be oppositionists. "I don't think we ever will be 100 percent for it. We're not 100 percent for anything, really. There are always a few stragglers over there who can't understand it."

But there are enough who do get it who are making cannabis the fastest growing industry in the United States. And it is an opportune time to launch a brand informed by all the positives cannabis offers. Willie's Reserve is billed as "a trailblazing line of marijuana products that celebrate Willie's love of cannabis and the culture surrounding it."

It is also a social statement. Willi says he started the company in part to prove a point. "I felt like if you really believe in something, why not promote it?"

Besides promoting wellness and recreation, Willie's Reserve will be an avenue to pursue environmental and social issues. When the company launched, spokesman Michael Bowman explained, that Willie wants it "to be something that's reflective of his passion. Ultimately, it's his, but it was developed by his family, and their focus [is] on environmental and social issues, and this crazy War on Drugs and trying to be a bright light amongst this trail as we're trying to extract ourselves from the goo of prohibition."

Willie's Reserve also provides a platform for another cause near to the singer's heart: to keep the cannabis industry's traditions of supporting local growers and mom-and-pop entrepreneurs by opposing Big Pot, the term used to describe the commercial takeover of marijuana.

Even though federal bans still exist, the states lining up to legalize medical and recreations have reached the tipping point. The swell of public opinion will continue to drive ever more states to legalize cannabis in some form. Initially "legit" businesses shied away because there was—and still is—a legal risk. The government could try to crack down against states' wishes. But with each new state that passes legislation, the more unlikely a national crackdown becomes.

So, more and more investors are looking for opportunities through various potential business models. One such model is licensing. In November 2016, Privateer Holdings, a Seattle-based private equity firm focused on cannabis industry investments, announced it was the first company in the cannabis industry to raise more than $100 million. Privateer, founded by three Silicon Valley entrepreneurs, have persuaded Bob Marley's family to license his name and image for their packaging. Using this licensing model, Privateer could first roll out legal products such as body lotions using the Marley name and image to build brand awareness before moving into cannabis products.

Another model is dubbed the Starbucks plan. Former Microsoft exec and tech millionaire, Jamen Shively announced plans in 2013 to create a chain of pot shops modeled on Starbucks through Diego Pellicer, a retail brand he co-founded. Specifically, the goal was to acquire retail space and then lease it or sublease it to local cannabis companies. At one point Shively announced, "We are Big Marijuana."

Diego Pellicer CEO, Ron Throgmartin (who replaced Shively as the public face of the company) stated, "We do not, and will not, profit from the sale of marijuana until it's federally legal to do so. As we wait, this company stands on solid real-estate principles. We will secure the real estate, we will lease the real estate, we will do the build out, and we have a future acquisition agreement that allows us to roll their operation into Diego Pellicer Worldwide. When it becomes federally legal to do so, we have the ability to acquire them overnight."

And then there is the small grower model represented by Willie's Reserve, a national holding company that extends its brand to one small company in each state that agrees to abide by a list of growing and purity standards. These companies either grow their own marijuana or source it from smaller farmers in the state.

Small growers are traditionally very environmentally conscious. When they were putting the company together, Willie told his partners, "I really believe in the environmental aspect of this. It's a great way to revitalize small farms, and I want to make sure that any product we grow is as clean as we can make it and that, wherever possible, we're trying to lower the environmental impact of our operations."

Quality and purity may be the first victims of Big Pot. Local growers use organic practices to ensure a clean, healthy product. NORML founder Keith Stroup says big companies tend to use chemicals.

"For the average little black-market grower, it's done on such a small scale that they're not even using pesticides," Stroup explained to *New York Magazine*. "But when you're investing millions of dollars in a large cultivation center, you can bet they are not going to take the risk of their crop getting wiped out by mold or mildew or insects."

A reporter who spent time with Willie in 2015 noted, "He really hadn't started the company for his own amusement, or to make money, of which he has plenty. The truth was that he wanted to preserve his legendary stash—to keep it clean, keep his growers in business, and keep Big Pot off his turf. He wanted to protect the plant he smokes every day from the corporate influence he's been fighting all his life."

Willie's assessment of Big Pot is a little more blunt. "They're trying to monopolize it all. That's horseshit. That ain't right, and we'll do everything we can to keep that from happening."